AMERICA'S CRISIS
AT THE BEGINNING OF THE THIRD MILLENNIUM

by

Rodolfo F. Saenz

authorHOUSE®

AuthorHouse™
1663 Liberty Drive, Suite 200
Bloomington, IN 47403
www.authorhouse.com
Phone: 1-800-839-8640

First published by AuthorHouse 11/6/2008

ISBN: 978-1-4389-1542-5 (sc)
ISBN: 978-1-4389-1541-8 (hc)

Library of Congress Control Number: 2008908353

Printed in the United States of America
Bloomington, Indiana

This book is printed on acid-free paper.

AMERICA'S CRISIS
AT THE BEGINNING OF THE THIRD MILLENNIUM

The Migration Crisis
The Energy Crisis
The Economic Recession
The Barack Obama Phenomenon
America and the Muslim Countries
Historical Roots and Related Stories

Rodolfo F. Saenz

Table of Contents

SECOND PART: HISTORICAL ROOTS

THIRD PART: RELATED STORIES

FOURTH PART: POETRY

Gratitude

I dedicate this book to my wife Agnes Giovanna Bartorelli, and to my children Gaston, Carmen Isabel, Agnes Giovanna and Marianella. I give them thanks for their support and help during the time I spent writing this book.

God bless you all.

Rodolfo F. Saenz

Acknowledgement

I give thanks to my son Gaston, and to my daughters Carmen Isabel, Agnes Giovanna and Marianella for their participation in the review of the draft of this book.

Rodolfo F. Saenz

To the Readers of this Book

"AMERICA'S CRISIS AT THE BEGINNING OF THE THIRD MILLENNIUM" is my first book in English. This book takes into consideration many historical facts and the influence that they have had in today's America situation, including the migration crisis, the energy crisis, America relations with the Muslin countries, and the economic recession.

Another important crisis that we have today in America is the environmental crisis, which is briefly covered in this book, but not with the extension that it deserves. The environmental crisis is not a crisis of America only, it is a crisis of the whole world and it is related to the survival of humankind in this planet; it requires a detailed and holistic consideration and analysis that is out of the scope of this book.

I am not a Professional Historian; I am a Professional Engineer. However, History has been my hobby and my passion during my whole life; maybe because my father was a professor of history when I was a child and in those days I read many of the books of History that he had at home.

This book must not be seen as an important research or as a professional work in History; the lack of detailed references says that clearly, but I believe that what is said in it is logic and close to reality. This book is more a child of my heart than a product of my mind, I do not have the capacity to demonstrate in a professional historical way everything I have written, but I believe that what I have written is important.

This book is not a novel, but I prefer that professional historians, if they have time to read it, look at it as if they were reading a novel. Traditionally, professional historians are specialists that write about specific issues after very serious research. Their works have many references.

An old definition says that a specialist is a person that every day knows more about less and at the end, this person knows almost everything about almost nothing; and that in the other hand, a generalist is a person that everyday knows less about more and at the end, this person knows almost nothing about almost everything. Scientists, with the exception of the ones like Leonardo da Vinci, look like specialists. Politicians and news media people look like generalists.

In the **FIRST** and **SECOND PARTS** of this book I made an effort to mention historical facts that really happened, and an effort has been made to interpret the consequences of these facts.

In the *Related Stories* of the **THIRD PART**, I mentioned historical facts that probably happened, but more literary freedom is used. This part has been written as a group of separated stories that are related to the general scope of the book. In the **FOURTH PART** some poetry is presented.

Something About Words and People

I lived in a suburb where I had two neighbors that became my friends, one who was a citizen from the Republic of India and the other was a Native American that I called the Indian. One day my wife left me a message telling me that the Indian neighbor wanted to talk with me, and I did not understand to whom of my two friends she was referring.

Christopher Columbus was lost when he arrived to the Americas. He thought that he had found India and called the aboriginal people he saw "Indians" and this was the name given to them by the Europeans for a long time. For this reason, the British called the Caribbean Islands West Indies.

In this book, I will use the term "Native Americans" when I mention the aboriginal people of the Americas, because I believe that the word "Indian" is the right one to refer to a citizen of the Republic of India.

Traditionally, the Eskimos were not included in the word "Indians", but now we can call them "Native Americans" because they are the Native Americans of Alaska and other very cold areas of America.

A "Mestizo" is a person with European and Native American background. The population of many Latin American countries has a high percentage of Mestizos. Many Native American women survived the Native American men killed in wars or hard work and had children with Spaniards. Many Spaniards came to America single or without their wives. Some of the people of mixed races look as if they had only one of the races. In other people, it is evident that they have a mixture of races.

In the Latin American families, when one of the children has his/her skin darker than that of his/her siblings he/she is called "el Negro" or "la Negra" that in Spanish means the person with a darker skin. This is a friendly term in Spanish, and people like to be called that way. Many wives call their husbands "mi Negro" as a synonymous of "my love." Likewise, many husbands call their wives "mi Negra." Some people that do not know this fact could feel offended to hear the word "Negro" or "Negra" because its sound is similar to "Nigger" that in English is considered offensive. Now that there are many recently arrived Spanish speakers in America it is important that the Americans understand that "Negro" or "Negra" are good and friendly words in Spanish. Traditionally the Hispanic people are not racist people because Spain was for several centuries the mixing bowl of many races.

The original migrants from Europe to the English Colonies of America were White, Anglo Saxons and most of them were Protestants. The term "WASP" has been applied to them. But the term "WASP" is not used too much today. Many Catholic immigrants came to America from Germany and Ireland. And the term would be only "WAS". But later many immigrants came from Italy, Greece, and other non Anglo Saxon countries of Europe. Many Jewish people also came to America. The term "WASP" was almost forgotten. However sometimes it is used to remember the first immigrants to the English North American Colonies.

It is interesting to observe that Spanish people almost never went to the English Colonies. It is obvious why. Spain and

England were not good friends during the colonial days. After the Independence of the United States of America Spanish people almost never came to live in this Country because they had the Spanish speaking Colonies to go there.

A lot of people of Spanish and of Mestizo background were suddenly present in the United States of America when this Country took or acquired former Spanish Colonies. The ancestors of this people that have been called "Chicanos" or "Mexican Americans" were in what is now the territory of the United States of America before the first English arrived.

In Latin America an American is a person from any country of The Americas. In the United States of America an American is a Citizen of this Country. That is correct because the name of the Country is America. We have the United States of America as we have the United States of Mexico and the United States of Venezuela.

United States is the name for a federal political system, no the name of a Country. The United States of America is the only country that has the name of the continent where it belongs. There is not a country with the name Europe, Asia, Africa or Oceania. Antarctica is a continent that does not have countries because there are not permanent inhabitants there.

In this book we will use the word "Americans" to refer to the Citizens of the United States of America.

FIRST PART: THE CRISIS

1 The Migration Crisis

In North America there are three big countries: The United States of America, Canada and Mexico.

Canada has too much territory in relation to its population. It has English and French influence. It is a very important country and very rich in natural resources. Canada has important immigration, but it does not have a migration or population situation with the complications that we see in Mexico and in the United States of America. At the beginning of the third millennium the population density of these three countries which became members of NAFTA (North America Free Trade Agreement) is:

Country	Inhabitants/sq. mile
Canada	9
United States of America	79
Mexico	145

Studying this table we can ask: why the Mexicans do not go to Canada?

One answer could be that the Mexicans do not like Canada because it is too cold for them.

Other answer is that the Mexicans do not go to Canada because it is too far.

But there are many Mexicans in cold areas of the United States of America far from Mexico.

A better answer is that the Mexicans do not go to Canada because they do not find there the jobs that they can find in the United States of America.

Many people in Mexico have had difficulties to find jobs with a salary that allow them to have the quality of life they want. On the other hand in the United States of America, which has a very strong economy, there are many companies that have difficulty hiring the labor force they need. The consequence of this situation is a heavy migration from Mexico to the United States of America.

The United States of America is a country of immigrants and it has been a melting pot where all the immigrants become Americans after some years in the country. Sometimes the immigrants have had difficulty learning to speak English well. But almost always the children of the immigrants learn to speak English very well. The immigrants and the children of immigrants have made great contributions to this country. Thomas Alba Edison, the American genius, that gave the light and many other things to us and to the world, was a son of immigrants.

At the beginning of the third millennium there was a new immigration situation caused by the presence of twelve million of undocumented immigrants in the United States of America; many people said that there could be fifteen million of undocumented immigrants in this Country. These immigrants are from Asia, Europe, Africa, South and Central America, but mainly from the neighbor country Mexico. It is estimated that every year the number of undocumented immigrants increases in more than 500,000 persons. The number of the undocumented immigrants that arrive per year is in the order of 750,000, and the number that is send back to their countries is in the order or 250,000.

In the year 2007 the Congress of the United States of America considered how to handle this situation but did not arrive to a law to fix it. The immigration issue was also well discussed in the magazines, newspapers, television, radio and all the media in general. This problem is becoming painful and is dividing America.

Some State legislatures, frustrated by the low progress that the Congress of the United States of America is making in the handling of this problem at the Federal level, are trying to solve it at State level, through legislation that would make illegal to give jobs, rent houses, give drivers licenses, and bring many government services, including health services, to the undocumented immigrants.

Some City and County governments are also taking some steps to participate in the management of the immigration situation. The problem with this policy is that local authorities will soon start to look for people in the streets, in the work places, in the churches, in the theaters, in the stadiums, etc. Like in any totalitarian state, citizens will become informants to the Authorities on the immigration status of people. Many American Citizens will need to walk out of home with their passports. This country will change forever if things continue this way. There is a high risk for racial profiling and hate crimes.

It is a big error to take the undocumented immigrants out of the public health services because the germs that cause many communicable diseases attack in the same way all people. If the undocumented immigrants do not receive the medical treatment they need, their untreated diseases will spread to all the population.

Ideas to Solve the Immigration Problems of the United States of America

Many ideas have been proposed to manage this situation; among them are the following:

- More Border Guards
- A wall
- A Guest Workers Program
- Improve the US Citizenship and Immigration Services (USCIS)
- A Program to Teach English to the Immigrants
- A Plan to Give a Visa to the undocumented Immigrants
- A Plan to Promote that Immigrants Become Permanent Residents
- A Program to Help the Permanent Residents to Become Citizens

All the ideas have a common objective: To stop the illegal immigration and to assimilate the immigrants that are here already and want to continue here.

Through the discussions we have learned that the country is divided about immigration. There are people who want the immigrants, and there are people who do not want them. There are people who like the immigrants and people who do not like them. There are people who love the immigrants and people who do not love them.

Traditionally the American people welcome newcomers. Almost everyone recognizes that this is a country of immigrants that accepts them.

There are some people who do not like the immigrants. There are several reasons. One of the reasons is that there are many new immigrants that came to this Country illegally. Other reason is that there have been some criminals, even some criminal gangs, between the immigrants. But the reality is that in any community of more than twelve million people there are criminals.

The Government of the United States of America is tough with the American criminals, and of course, it has to be very tough with the immigrants that become or are criminals.

There are some people who do not like the new immigrants because many of them are Native Americans or "Mestizos." They forget, or do not know, that they are the children of the Native Americans that have lived in The Americas for several millenniums. The reason for this is that they do not know them well, because they have not been in contact with them before. It is possible that the reduced number of Native Americans in the United States of America, the American system of Reservations for Native Americans, and some old western Hollywood movies about "Indians" has something to do with this attitude.

More Guards in the Border between Mexico and the United States of America

Almost everybody agrees that it is convenient and necessary to improve the border's control. More Border Guards are necessary. Better facilities and better equipment are required.

Modern methods of surveillance and monitoring can help to control the borders better.

In the year 2007 the Government of the United States of America employed more than 13,000 Border Patrol Agents; there are approved plans to increase their number to 18,000 at the end of 2008.

But to improve the control of only one border will no help too much. It is necessary to improve simultaneously the control of the border with Canada and all the coasts of the United States of America. The drug smugglers and the people's smugglers or "coyotes" will not abandon their activities easily.

The increase in the number of the Border Guards is only part of the solution. It has to be accompanied with sanctions to the companies that hire illegal immigrants, and the overhaul of the U.S. Citizenship and Immigration Service (USCIS) to facilitate the legal entrance to the country of the persons that are necessary to complete the manpower that the Country needs.

The increment in the number and in the efficiency of the Border Patrol Agents will help to stop the activities of the Volunteer Border Patrols and its inconveniences.

The Volunteer Border Patrols

Many Americans who live in properties close to the border with Mexico are disappointed because their farms are frequently invaded. Sometimes the smugglers of people or coyotes and the immigrants with them take food from these farms and may damage the crops and facilities. In some cases they can take cattle and poultry.

The farmers have organized volunteer border patrols to protect their land and to avoid that the coyotes and those traveling with them trespass their properties. The farmers say that because the Federal Government of the United States of America is not protecting well our borders, they have to do it, at least in the areas close to their properties.

We can say that the members of these volunteer border patrols are good people. They want to protect their equity for which they have worked hard all their lives. But what they are doing is dangerous.

When the members of these patrols have been in the border area for a long time, they understand better the complexity of the situation. However, when the members of the patrols are new comers or recent immigrants from other continents, they are prone to make serious mistakes more often.

Despite that the Border Patrols of the Government of the United States of America have been well trained, sometimes they make mistakes. Sometimes Border Patrol agents have to apologize to people they interrogate after realizing that they are not undocumented immigrants. The volunteer patrols that act without adequate training in how to use firearms safely and conduct this type of operations could make mistakes and be involved in serious accidents, with bad consequences for everyone. Sometimes it is not easy to know the difference between a person who just came to America illegally and one who belongs to an ethnic group that has been in America for centuries or millenniums.

There are many citizens of the United States of America with Spanish last names (i.e. Rodriguez, Morales, Fernandez, Jimenez, etc.) who have never been in Mexico. Some of them belong to Native American communities and got their Spanish names when their ancestors where baptized by Spanish missioners many centuries ago. The Spanish missioners had long lists with Spanish names and asked the natives what name they would like. That happened in North America, in Central America, in South America, and in the Philippines. It is interesting to note, that Native Americans of areas where the Spanish people explorers never went have names that in many cases describe the translation into English of their original native names (i.e. Fasthorse, Bigfoot, Greycloud, Redcloud, Carefoot, etc.).

In the States that have a border with Mexico (California, Arizona, New Mexico, and Texas) there are many families with Spanish last names whose ancestors were living in those states when they became part of the United States of America. These families never traveled to America. They were swallowed by America.

The members of the volunteer border patrols think that they may easily identify a group of undocumented immigrants and their coyotes because they are supposed to have a special attitude and look afraid and nervous. However, if a group of American youngsters is having a picnic and they find out that a patrol is approaching them with their firearms, they may also look afraid and nervous. Many Hispanic Americans or Native Americans, who use to work making deliveries to properties close to the border with Mexico, have abandoned their jobs because they are afraid of the members of the volunteer border patrols and do not want to go to the properties on the border area. They do not feel safe there and are afraid of the firearms of the patrols. The Government of the United Sates of America must improve the control of the borders and these volunteer border patrols must abandon their activities.

A Wall between Mexico and the United States of America

"Mr. Gorvachev, tear down this wall." Ronald Reagan, Berlin, June 12, 1987.

The people of Latin America remember with nostalgia the days of President Franklin D. Roosevelt and its "Good Neighbor Policy;" and the days of President John F. Kennedy and its "Alliance for Progress."

Today the United States of America is the country that is building a wall in its border with Latin America. The 88 miles fence that exists in the southwest border is going to be increased with a 700 miles border fence. And there are many People and many Congressmen that want more walls.

It looks that the American Government forgot Latin America. The Latin American politicians that are pro the United States of America are not winning elections, as happened recently in Venezuela, Bolivia, Ecuador, Nicaragua and other Latin

American countries. It almost happened also in Mexico, Peru and Costa Rica in the last elections. Many Latin Americans see now the United States of America as the Country that is building a wall because it does not like them.

It looks that some American Congressmen believe that a wall is the solution for everything, and they are disappointed because the wall is not being built as soon, as long and as high as they would like.

A wall is not a new idea. It is an old idea. The Chinese have the China wall, the longest wall ever built, since many centuries ago. The French built the Maginot Line before the Second World War and it was demonstrated that it was unhelpful. The Soviets built the infamous **Berlin Wall**.

Walls are built when it is not possible to get security in a more civilized way.

During the Middle Age, known to historians as the Dark Age, many walls were built. In many developing countries the landscape is ruined by the great quantity of walls surrounding the houses and buildings.

Developed free countries build bridges to unite people, not walls to separate them. To build a wall in the border between Mexico and the United States of America in this time of globalization and the North America Free Trade Agreement is an anachronism.

Even if we build a long wall in the whole border with Mexico, it will not stop the smugglers of drugs and people. Are we going to build walls in the Pacific Coast, in the Gulf Coast or in the Atlantic Coast? Are we going to build a wall in the border with Canada?

The small portions of the border wall already built demonstrated that it would be an ecological disaster. The wild animals that live in the border do not know if they are Mexican or if they are Americans. Many of them had perished because they need to go to both sides of the border for food, water and to get the habitat they need.

A Guest Workers Program

Most American families are small in size. They only have one or two children. The parents work hard for their children. They educate them very well. They save money to be able to send them to college that now is very expensive. They are very good parents, and what they do is very good. But there are many jobs that these college educated people would not like to take, but that somebody has to do. Many new immigrants want to take these jobs.

In the United States of America there are many seniors that need assistance and demand services. Many immigrants are helping these old people. Many young immigrants are taking jobs that many middle age or old persons do not want to do.

If all the undocumented immigrants that live today in the United States stop working suddenly, it would be a crisis for the economy. They work in agriculture, in construction, in transportation, in the meat and poultry industry, in restaurants, in housekeeping and institutional cleaning, security, etc.

Most of the immigrants work hard to improve their education level, their knowledge of the English language and their immigration status with the idea to move to better jobs. In the past, when they moved to better jobs their former jobs were taken by new undocumented immigrants. But we want to change this. Part of the solution could be a guest worker's program.

In this program the guest workers will come to the country legally, but only for a limited time. The idea is to give them a time to live with a better salary, improve their education and study English, but then return to their original country. In this way the United States of America stops the illegal immigration, and Mexico and other countries do not lose their citizens and their contributions. The idea is to change a situation of illegal migration into a bilateral cooperation program through negotiations with the Government of Mexico and other interested countries.

The guest Workers Program is a good idea. But it is difficult to determine the amount of guest workers that are needed and that it is convenient to authorize. The enemies of the Guest Workers Program say that the guests will no go back to Mexico and will stay in the United States of America as new undocumented immigrants.

Improve the US Citizenship and Immigration Services (USCIS)

Many people that want to come to this country legally are sick and tired of waiting for the USCIS resolutions; sometimes they lose their hope and take the decision to become undocumented immigrants.

After the September eleven (of the year 2001) attacks the former Immigration and Naturalization Service (INS) and the United States Citizenship and Immigration Services (USCIS) have gone even slower than before. The majority of the suicide air pirates that made the attack of September eleven were legal immigrants. One green card was sent to one of them after he killed himself in this attack.

Now the USCIS has to check who comes into this country better than before. The problem is that while the Immigrations Services check, many illegal immigrants come.

The former INS and the USCIS were not designed to work fast and supply the hundreds of thousands of workers that the growing and strong American Economy needs. The Citizenship and Immigration Services needs to be improved. This improvement will help to get the hundreds of thousands of persons that are needed and want to come legally to work in this country; it will help the family reunion programs and it is also the necessary complement of the Guest Workers Program.

A Program to Teach English to the Immigrants

Lack of the English language knowledge is a serious problem with either legal or undocumented immigrants. If they do not speak English they isolate themselves with the people of their same language and do no integrate and do no interact with rest of the population.

Many private companies and community organizations had made efforts to teach English to their employees that are immigrants. There have been bill proposals in Congress to authorize the Federal Government of the United States of America to finance more programs to teach English to the immigrants. These are very good proposals.

In the City of Rockville, Maryland, there is an organization named Community Ministries of Rockville that established a program called Latino Outreach Program. It was a success. It helps the small children with childcare and homework assistance while their parents take the English classes. These children participate also in musical activities and tobacco use prevention programs. The program also enrolls the participants in community health programs. It coordinates its efforts with the Latino Health Initiative of Montgomery County. It has also a course for the adult participants that want to become Citizens of the United States of America.

In the last Latino Outreach Program Graduation more than 200 adult students finished the program, and more than 150 children attended the tutoring program.

Private companies support this program and ask their employees who are immigrants to improve their English in it. The companies that support this program say that their contributions are good investments because they recover them with the better behavior and productivity of the employees after they speak English well.

The Montgomery County Government and the City of Rockville Government support Community Ministries of Rockville programs and contribute to their expenses. They know that these are good investments for the Local Government.

As the Executive Director Emeritus of Community Ministries of Rockville, the Reverend Mansfield Kaseman says, "thanks to programs like this the City of Rockville is a better place to live". If we could organize this kind of programs in many communities of this country "the United States of America would be a better place to live." Maybe in the future programs like these could get support of the State and Federal Government. Recently the Supreme Court of the United States of America decided that it is possible to use Federal Government resources to support social programs sponsored by religious organizations.

A Plan to Give a Visa to the Undocumented Immigrants

The public opinion is divided in regarding a proposal to give a visa to the undocumented immigrants as a first step prior to accept them as permanent residents and to give them a "green card".

The opponents to this visa say that this is a country of law and that the undocumented people must be sent back home. But they forget that the companies that hired the undocumented immigrants were involved also in an illegal activity. What will happen to these companies? We travel through the roads and live in homes built or repaired with the participation of the undocumented immigrants, and eat the poultry or the meat packed by them. Are we also involved in illegal activities? Is the U.S Federal Government who knows that they are here and allows them to stay involved also in an illegal activity?

Many of the opponents to the visa program say that this visa will be an amnesty to help people that have broken the law and that they deserve deportation. They are also critics of the people that help the undocumented immigrants. They are wrong. Traditionally the people of the United States of America have been kind to the pilgrims and immigrants. They helped them to learn the English language; they helped them to get jobs and to organize their lives in their new Country. The enforcement of the immigration laws is a responsibility of the Federal Government. But after the people are here what we have are people helping people. It has to be that way, and it has been always that way in a country were people know that the best way to be close to God is helping our neighbors, the pilgrims and the people in our communities.

The supporters of the visa proposal say that it would be a disaster for the economy to send all the undocumented immigrants back home, and that it is physically impossible anyway. They also say that Congress can establish sanctions for having come illegally to this country, like a fine or longer terms to become citizens and not necessarily jail or deportation.

Lawyers know that the concept of legal or illegal is a relative concept. The occupation of the Americas by the Europeans was illegal. For the English of those days the American Revolution was illegal. For a long time slavery was legal and a run-away slave was committing an illegal action.

All the countries have legislative powers because they can change the law or adapt the law to the social needs and changing situations. Congress represents the will of the people, and what it decides is legal in any organized society in a given territory. This is why the law is called "the law of the land."

To deport all the undocumented immigrants could be legal but it is not morally correct and is not practical. When the immigrants are undocumented it is not easy to take them and put them in the border with Mexico, because in many cases the United States of America authorities do not know what are the nationalities of the immigrants. These Authorities have to demonstrate to the Mexican Authorities that they are Mexicans before sending them back. In the case of immigrants from farther countries the deportation would be more complicated because of the travel involved.

A Plan to Promote that the Immigrants Become Permanent Residents

Most of the undocumented immigrants have worked hard to have their homes and other goods. Many of them have children that are citizens of the United States of America. If the immigrants continue here, it is wise to give them the opportunity to become permanent residents of this Country.

17

Currently, permanent residents have held their green card for five years before they can apply for its citizenship. There are some proposals to make this period longer for undocumented immigrants as a punishment because they came to this country illegally.

A Program to Help the Permanent Residents to Become Citizens

The citizenship is important because it provides the maximum immigration rights available in the United States of America and gives the immigrants the right to vote and facilitates their participation in the community discussions and the American Political process.

After becoming U.S. citizens they become more rapidly a part of the American melting pot, and of the American dream. This is very important in a country that does not want to have citizens of second class.

To become citizens of the United States of America, the immigrants have to study the history of this country, how the government system works; and what are the responsibilities of this society toward the Local, State and Federal levels of the Government.

Conclusions

Few issues have divided the people and Congress of the United States of America as the issue of immigration. The risk of doing nothing is a great risk and the situation could be worst every day.

The most important steps that the United States of America has to take to solve the immigration crisis are:

Secure the borders including the coastlines; but not only the border with Mexico, and not with walls. There are more civilize ways to secure the borders than walls.

Accept that there are many American companies that do not get all the manpower they need and that people from other countries have to come to fill that need. It is better for the country, the American workers and the immigrants that they come here legally. This is why a guest workers program is convenient.

It is not convenient that the twelve million of undocumented immigrants living in the United States of America continue with that status. The undocumented immigrants have broken the law, but also the United States of America have broken the law by allowing them to stay here knowing that they are here. Some American companies have also broken the law by giving them jobs.

Amnesty is not convenient. At the same time Congress has the power to punish the immigrants for breaking the law without deportation. A solution to this situation has to be found. Some possible solutions are the following:

Give a visa to the undocumented immigrants in order to identify them. This will facilitate the necessary immigration control, including knowledge about where they are and what they are doing.

Promote that the immigrants become permanent residents. But fine them when they get their green card for coming illegally to the country.

Promote that the permanent residents become U.S. citizens, but process differently those who came to the country illegally. For example, they could need a period longer than five years holding the green card, as a punishment for coming illegally to America, before they can apply for U.S. citizenship.

Improve the capacity of the US Citizenship and Immigration Services (USCIS) to facilitate the arrival of legal immigrants into the country, including skill workers, immigrant family members to promote the reunion of divided families, etc. USCIS should also increase its capacity to handle all the cases intended to solve the immigration crisis efficiently.

The United States of America should increase its vegetative rate of population growth to lower its dependency on immigrants, to have a younger population and to solve some problems that an old population creates in social security, retirement programs and in the society in general.

A woman who is bringing a new child to a community is giving the best that can be given to it. She is also doing the best that she can do for her country. She deserves all the necessary help and support. More support is needed for the parents, mothers, babies and young children. If we do not stimulate our own growth of population, and do not facilitate legal immigration, more undocumented immigrants will come.

The rate of abortion should be reduced through more counseling services and more support for the potential mothers that are thinking in abortion. More programs for adoption of children whose mothers could not take care of them should be established. It is estimated that in the most recent years, more than one million of abortion have been performed per year in the United States of America. It is also estimated that more than half million of undocumented immigrants have been coming to this country every year. We can say that by closing the borders and by reducing the number of abortions to the half, the United States of America would continue with the same population increase. Of course the new half million of children will not solve the problem of required manpower immediately, but it will in the long term.

The Federal and State Governments should increase the tax benefits to the parents and to the people that are taking care of children to a level closer to the real cost of raising children.

2 The Energy Crisis

Level of Development and Consumption of Energy

The developed industrialized world works hard to elevate the standard of living of its people. This effort requires the consumption of great amounts of energy. Despite the negative environmental impact of energy consumption, there is a correlation between the level of development and the consumption of energy and between the quality of life, in accordance with the parameters we use to measure it, and the consumption of energy. The most advanced countries are also the ones that consume more energy per capita.

There is also a correlation between the consumption of energy and the quality of the environment, and specifically between the consumption of energy and the air quality. The plants that burn coal are the most used in the United States of America to generate electricity. One of the major concerns about air pollution is the burning of coal to generate electricity, despite that there are modern power plants that burn coal producing less air pollution than the old ones. Other electric plants, that burn natural gas, bunker, diesel and other fuels of fossil origin are also important air polluters. In addition to the environmental problem originated by fuels consumption we have to consider also the environmental impact produced by the industry of oil, carbon and other fossil fuels extraction and transportation.

Many Latin American Governments invited American companies to explore their energetic resources and develop their oil production industry. Many of the political leaders that invited these companies lost the support of the people mainly for the lack of concern that these companies had for the environmental protection, the evaluation of the environmental impact of their activities and for their lack of interest in the well being of the inhabitants of the oil producing areas.

Despite all the environmental concerns that we have about energy consumption and extraction we have to understand and accept that we have created a "civilization" that is based in energy consumption and that it is not easy to change it suddenly; what we can do is to try to correct this situation with gradual technological adjustments in energy use, better social concern about the fate of the people affected by the modern industrial activities, and a better evaluation and correction of the environmental impacts of fuels extraction, transportation and consumption.

Planet Earth, with almost seven billion people pushing for economic growth in order to achieve a high quality of life is being subject to an amount of energy consumption never imagined before; and of course, to an environmental deterioration that could destroy the Planet. This is what former Vice-President of the United States of America Albert Gore has called "an inconvenient true".

We must change the world present path. But this is not the scope of this chapter. The scope of this chapter is about how we can solve the present energy crisis of the United States of America.

At the beginning of the third millennium the United States of America is facing a problem that is becoming critical. It does not produce all the oil that it needs in its own territory. It has to import more than sixty percent of the oil it consumes.

Unfortunately, some of the countries that sell the oil to the United States of America not always see this country as a good customer or as a friend. There are historical reasons for this attitude. American and other developed countries oil companies were directed and managed by business men who were mainly interested in the oil extraction and in the rate of return of their investments; they hired many engineers, economists, administrators, and technicians who worked in the countries that have the oil resources. The leaders of the oil companies had not a great concern for environmental protection or for the fate of the people of the oil producing countries; they did not hire enough environmentalists, sociologists, social workers, anthropologists or historians to know more about the people where they were working, their wishes and their culture. The oil companies established good relations with the country's governments; but several times the political situations changed, as happened in Iran, Iraq and Venezuela, and the relations with the oil producing countries became complicated.

When we fill up our car fuel tank, or pay our energy bills, we know that part of that money could go to some countries that could not like us.

Our Oil Suppliers

In the United States of America the imported oil comes from many countries. The most important are: Mexico, Venezuela, Saudi Arabia, Iraq and Kuwait. Here are some comments:

Mexico, it is considered a friendly country, but it is the country with which we are building the border wall. Mexico is growing too fast and every year it needs more oil for its own consumption and has less oil to export.

Venezuela, it is the country of President Hugo Chaves, the great friend of the Cuba's communist government, who does not like the United States of America.

Saudi Arabia, it is the country of a friendly government but the birthplace of most of the Muslin extremist suicide air pirates that attacked us on September eleven of 2001.

Iraq, the country of the unfriendly late dictator Sadam Hussein; this is the country that the United States of America invaded, occupied and is trying to help to fix its chaotic situation.

Kuwait, it is considered a friendly country, it is the country that Iraq's Sadam Hussein invaded and the United Nations, in cooperation with the United States of America, liberated in the First Gulf War.

The world oil supply situation is aggravated by the fact that China and India, the two most populated countries of the world have increased their consumption of oil and other energetic products in the last years. Some countries that today sell oil to the United States of America are looking for other markets.

There is not a guarantee that the required imported oil will continue to flow to the United States of America forever.

Because of the high demand, the price of oil is going up worldwide. This is a source of inflation because transportation costs and energy costs are components of the cost of almost everything. We have seen that because of the high price of gasoline, the prices of homes, and its air conditioning equipments and appliances have gone up in the last years. The prices of food and the restaurant's menus prices are also going up.

The positive aspect of the high prices of gasoline is that some people are driving fewer miles per month, reducing the demand of oil, producing less air pollution and doing more exercise.

Other Energetic Possibilities

From the energetic point of view, the United States of America is a vulnerable country. It is obvious that this Country has to do something to change this situation. But what can we do?

One possibility to handle this problem is to increase the use of other sources of energy, such as: nuclear energy, wind energy, solar energy, hydroelectric energy, geothermal energy, bio fuels and ethanol, transformation of coal to liquid gas, use of electric vehicles, use of natural gas in transportation, and use of hydrogen as a fuel.

These and other technologies can help to import less fuels and oil. However, it is not possible to say that we can stop the use of oil and other fossil fuels suddenly and completely. This is why the exploration for more fossil fuels, including oil and natural gas, still must be considered as very important and necessary activities.

Nuclear Energy

Nuclear energy constitutes one of the most important resources we have to solve the energy crisis. Nuclear energy is clean because it does not send emissions to the atmosphere, like the power plants that burn coal. On the other hand, there is a problem with the disposal of the radioactive wastes. They constitute an environmental problem and it is not easy to find a safe place were to bury them. There is also a problem of security with these wastes. They must be buried in a high security place were no terrorists or enemies could reach them, because these wastes can be used to make a dirty bomb (a bomb that can spread radioactive substances). Some of these wastes contain a portion of plutonium that could be used to make atomic weapons.

While France produces about eighty percent of its electric energy from nuclear power plants, the United States of America produces only about twenty percent. Furthermore, after the Three Mile Island accident in Pennsylvania, nobody in America wants a new nuclear power plant close to his/her house or town. But the American people have to understand that it is safer for the United States of America to have more nuclear power plants than to continue with the emissions of the power plants that burn coal, and with the dependency of imported fuels from some countries that do not see us as a friend.

If the nuclear energy industry and the government of the United States of America can demonstrate and convince the people of America, that we can increase the percentage of electricity generated with nuclear power with absolute safety in the power plants and absolute safety in the management of nuclear fuels and in the disposal of the nuclear wastes, we would be closer to the solution of the energy crisis. If France can generate eighty percent of its electricity with nuclear energy, we should do something similar.

Wind Energy

There are many parts in the world where the winds represent a source of energy. The equipments used to transform wind energy into electric energy have improved a lot in recent years.

We can see now many wind mill generators in several windy parts of the United States of America and of the World. Wind energy, also called eolic energy is present only in specific windy areas. It can help, but in a limited way compared to the total amount of energy required. Wind energy is good business for the people that are producing and using it.

Solar Energy

Solar energy has the advantage that it is available anywhere. Where there is not cold weather, like in tropical areas, the sun energy can be used directly to heat water circulating it through coils that are put in the roof of the houses.

The sun energy can also be gotten through the use of panels of photoelectric cells that can produce electricity from the light of the sun. If these panels are put in the roofs of the houses, they will take less electricity from the public system and the electricity bills will go down. In some cases electricity can be sent to the public system.

Solar energy is very important in isolated areas where there are not power lines and where the panels of photoelectric cells combined with batteries can bring light and power during the night.

Hydroelectric Energy

Hydroelectric energy is clean because hydroelectric plants do not send emissions to the atmosphere, and they constitute a permanent source of energy. Hydroelectric plants are very expensive and require great investments of capital. Almost all the available hydraulic resources have been developed in industrialized countries, like in the United States of America, the European countries and Japan. Consequently, it is not possible to talk of them as a new source of energy.

However, in the underdeveloped countries there is a big amount of hydraulic resources that have not been developed because they do not have the required capital. If the international financing agencies, like the World Bank or the Inter-American Development Bank, finance these countries to build more hydroelectric plants, it would help these countries a lot because they would consume less fossil fuel and less oil, which will be good for the rest of the world.

There are not concerns about air pollution with hydroelectric plants, but on the other hand, they have some effect in the water resources environment. They decrease the purification capacity of rivers; therefore, dams and reservoirs could have negative ecological consequences.

Another negative aspect of hydroelectric plants is that frequently they need reservoirs that inundate former agricultural lands and former human and wildlife habitats.

Geothermal Energy

There are many countries with geothermal resources that have not been developed. The situation is similar to the one explained in the case of hydroelectric power, the development of the geothermal resources requires high investments of capital. Because geothermal energy is not as abundant as the hydraulic energy, there is more difficult to find competent consultant companies with experience in this field of energy. Countries with many volcanoes such as Italy, Japan and the Central American countries have developed geothermal resources, not only for the generation of electricity, but also to heat factories, buildings, houses and other facilities.

Bio Fuels and Ethanol

To fuel vehicles with ethanol or other bio fuels is another possibility. This practice reduces the consumption of imported oil, and the vehicle emissions are less toxic. However, the growing demand for food worldwide will make difficult to use agricultural lands to produce crops for fuel production. The use of agricultural wastes to produce bio fuels or ethanol is a more interesting possibility.

Brazil produces great quantities of ethanol and this country is self sufficient in energy. Brazil gets its ethanol mainly from sugar cane. The United States of America produces some ethanol from corn, soy and other crops. The percentage of ethanol for vehicles that the United States of America produces is small compared with the total amount of oil consumed by this country.

It is possible to get more gallons of ethanol per acre per year with sugar cane than with corn or soy. To import ethanol from tropical countries is a very interesting possibility that could help the economies of those countries. However, that has to be done careful protecting the American industry of ethanol so that it does not create another dependency of imported energy.

The production of ethanol has negative environmental aspects, as could be de destruction of forests to produce crops used by the ethanol distilleries. The countries that produce ethanol have to be careful establishing policies that give priority to the production of food.

Ethanol for vehicles is always sold as a mixture with gasoline, because this mixture is good for the engines and to avoid the consumption of the ethanol by some irresponsible people.

In the countries where agriculture is an important activity and there is enough land and need for more jobs, the production of ethanol could help a lot the economy.

There are people that have concerns regarding the production of bio fuels and ethanol. They say that to change wild areas into cultivation areas to produce bio fuels will have negative consequences for the ecology. They also say that in countries with small territories the production of bio fuels could be a bad competition to the production of food. They believe that the production of ethanol could increase the cost of food for people.

Taking into consideration that the world population is growing to fast, and that the cost of food is increasing worldwide, it is possible that in the future the production of ethanol from agricultural areas crops will not be competitive. However, the production of ethanol and bio fuels from agricultural wastes could continue.

Transformation of Coal to Liquid Gas

Coal constitutes one of the best reserves of energetic substances that the United States of America has. Some studies indicate that at the actual rate of consumption the country has reserves of coal for more that two hundred years.

Coal is used to produce a great amount of the electricity generated in the United States of America. If more nuclear power plants were constructed to generate electricity, the reserves of coal would become bigger in relation to a lower consumption of coal for electricity. Here is where the production of liquid gas from coal to fuel vehicles has a great potential.

The technology for the production of liquid gas from coal is available. If this liquid gas were used to fuel vehicles it could reduce the importation of oil. There are states like Pennsylvania, Illinois, Kentucky, West Virginia and others that produce coal and see a great possibility in the production of liquid gas from coal. These are states that need to increase employment.

On the other hand, the emissions from vehicles fueled with liquid gas from coal could be more harmful than the emissions from the vehicles fueled with gasoline or ethanol. This is the reason why some environmentalist groups are opposed to this possibility.

If more nuclear plants were built, the emissions of the automobiles fueled with liquid gas from coal would be compensated with the reduction in the burning of coal to produce electricity.

If the technology to produce liquid gas from coal can be improved to get a cleaner fuel, or if we learn to design vehicle engines fueled with liquid gas from coal that produces cleaner emissions, we would be closer to the solution of the energy crisis we have.

Use of Electric Vehicles

The use of electric vehicles is a very interesting possibility because instead of going to the filling station to fill up your tank you would plug your car to your home electric wire net during the night. The next day your batteries would be fully charged.

The energy you would use in your vehicle would come from nuclear power plants, from plants that burn coal, or from hydroelectric plants. You would be consuming only a little bit of energy from imported oil. Your vehicle would not produce emissions, but it is possible that emissions were produced in some of the power plants that generated the electricity you use in your car.

Use of Natural Gas in Transportation

The use of natural gas in transportation can be a way to reduce the importation of oil. Natural gas is abundant in the United States of America and has been found in several countries of the world in resent years. Some of the countries that have discovered natural gas in their territories are looking for markets to export it.

Use of hydrogen as a fuel

Hydrogen is used as a fuel in rockets for space travel; but it can also be used as a fuel for vehicles. It has the advantage that the vehicles' emissions will be just water. The engines to use hydrogen as a fuel are expensive; the fuel is expensive, and there are several technical problems that need to be solved before a massive use of hydrogen as a fuel could be done.

Reduction of the Consumption of Energy

There are many actions that could be taken at various levels in order to reduce the consumption of energy.

The automobile and truck manufacturers should manufacture vehicles more efficient in fuel consumption. There are technologies that would allow the manufacturers to do so, however, the cost of a change to this technology is high, and the vehicles would be more expensive. Legislation was approved at the end of 2007 forcing the automobile and truck industry to take this step because in a competitive market no company can do this in an isolated way.

The manufacturers of power plants should construct plants with a higher energy efficiency and lower environmental pollution. This step would also require legislation taking into consideration the higher costs and higher investments that would be required.

The new houses and buildings have to be constructed with a better insulation. An effort to improve the insulation of the existing houses and buildings has to be done.

An important aspect in the solution of the energy problem is to educate people about the importance of reducing the consumption of energy. For example, in winter we could heat our homes at a lower temperature (66 degrees Fahrenheit) and wear sweaters. In summer we could cool our homes at higher temperature (73 degrees Fahrenheit). It is important to have houses with windows, walls and ceilings that are well insulated to reduce the cost of heating and air conditioning.

We could only turn on the lights of the areas where we are staying while at home or work, and use energy efficient light bulbs. When we cook, we have to know that after the water or the soup is boiling, we do not need the stove switch in the high position, it must be moved to the low position.

People could make more car pools and drive less. In some work places, they can accept flexible time that allows the employees not to drive in rush hours when the vehicles are less fuel efficient because of the heavy traffic.

People should try not to use their cars for short distances. It is better to walk. It is better for the people's health, for the environment and energy conservation.

Conclusions

The United States of America could solve the energy crisis that it has been facing at the beginning of the third millennium by taking the following steps:

Increment the amount of electricity generated by nuclear power plants.

Power more vehicles with liquid gas produced from coal.

Power more vehicles with bio fuels and ethanol, and use more electric vehicles.

Finance hydroelectric and geothermic projects overseas.

Continue the exploration for additional oil and natural gas.

Improve the fuel efficiency of automobiles, trucks and other vehicles.

Improve the insulation of houses and buildings.

Reduce the consumption of energy.

It is important to take into consideration that the measures mentioned before to solve the energy crisis have positive environmental aspects; however, they require an **environmental** complement that includes:

> Decommission of old coal burning electric power plants that are not energetically efficient and produce high pollution. Limit the construction of new coal burning plants, and construct only energetically and environmentally efficient new ones.

> Find a safe way for the transportation of nuclear fuels and nuclear wastes; and a safe place for the disposal of the nuclear wastes of the nuclear power plants.

> More research is necessary to make possible the manufacture of vehicles fueled with liquid gas from coal, which are more environmentally efficient.

In this chapter we have talked about a possible solution to the energy crisis. However, we are no saying that it is an easy one. It is a difficult one. But something has to be done. As the country grows, the dependence on imported oil could become worse.

The solution proposed probably would increase the price of the electricity for our houses and of the fuels for our cars. But at the same time this increase in price will facilitate the reduction in the consumption of energy. It is more difficult and more dangerous to have a country that is vulnerable in its energy supply and one that can be stopped by its foreign energy suppliers; a country which future could be with an anxiety similar to that of a car driver who does not know if he will find a gas station to fill his tank in an unknown road.

It is more difficult and more dangerous to continue with wars that could be related to the energy crisis, and sending our money to countries that do not see us as a friend.

3 America and the Muslim Countries

In the early days of the United States of America, the relations with the Muslim countries were almost inexistent. These countries were too far from America, and the Americans did not know much about the Muslims, their religion, traditions and culture.

When the Founder Fathers of America wrote documents about freedom of religion, they were probably thinking about the liberty of Christians to worship in the way they preferred, and about the liberty of agnostics and atheists to think in the way they wanted. When the constitution of the United States of America established that this was a secular country with freedom of conscience, all religions were made legal in the United States of America. When the first Jewish people came to America, they could worship and establish their Synagogues freely; and many years later when the first Muslim people came to America, they could also worship freely and establish their Mosques as well. The same fate has occurred in America with all the other religions that do not practice or sponsor illegal activities.

The Jewish, Christian, and Islamic religions deserve special consideration. The people who practice these religions believe in only one God, the God of Abraham. Traditionally, the Christians wanted the whole world to become Christian, and the Muslims wanted the whole world to become Islamic. These dreams about having only one religion worldwide gave origin to many wars and killings among people who worship the same God. The Jewish differ from Christians and Muslims in the fact that they do not seem to want that the whole world become Jewish; they consider their religion as their heritage, as the religion of the Jewish people, a group of people with a great tradition.

The desire for worldwide conquest of Christians and Muslims created the more than one millennium long conflict between the Europeans and the Middle East people. Because America is a country originally conquered by European immigrants, some Muslims, who remember the crusades and many other attacks from the West, see America as an enemy despite that Americans did not have contact with them and ignored them for many years, and despite the great geographical distance between America and the Muslim countries. Probably many Muslim people do not know that America was born as a country fighting European imperialism.

The wars between Christians and Muslims, known as religious wars, were in reality wars made by the politicians of different times, who used religion for their own purposes. Almost all religions want peace and love and recognize that the humanity is people with souls that are part of God. God wants the welfare and happiness of all people who are His creatures despite of what they believe or what their religion is.

Probably, one of the first contacts of America with Muslims happened in 1801 after some American merchant ships were attacked in the Mediterranean Sea. President Thomas Jefferson was informed that the attackers were Muslim pirates that had their base in Tripoli. From 1801 to 1805 America sent warships to Tripoli in several occasions. Finally, the ruler of Tripoli agreed to stop the attacks of his country ships against American ships.

In 1981, two fighter planes of the United States of America shut down two Libyan fighter planes that intercepted them in the Gulf of Sidra, which was claimed as Libya's national waters by Muammar Qaddafi's Libyan regime. In March of 1986, in another encounter, American Navy ships destroyed two Libyan ships in the Sidra gulf. America never accepted that other countries put limitations to its right to navigate in international waters.

In April 1986, President Ronald Reagan ordered attacks with plane bombers to Libya to respond to terrorist attacks of that country to American interests in Europe. In 1988, Libyan agents put a bomb in a Pan American Airlines jet that exploded in Scotland. At the request of the United States of America the United Nations applied sanctions to Libya when it refused to extradite the suspect perpetrators of the Pan American jetliner terrorist attack. After the sanctions, Libya changed its attitude, cooperated with the investigations about the Pan American airplane bomb, and became a more moderate country.

The discovery of great amounts of oil in the Muslim countries and the need of America to import great amounts of oil made possible that these distant countries became commercial partners. The establishment of strong diplomatic relations followed the commercial contacts and investments of American companies in Muslim countries.

Many leaders in Muslim countries see America as a client and as a partner in the development of their oil industry and had established good relations with America. However, there are some people in the Muslim countries who hate America and say that America is a country of infidels. There are also people that do not like the oil companies for their traditional lack of concern for environmental protection and for the fate of the native people living in the areas where they are working.

When the United Nations recognized the State of Israel in 1948, the United States of America also recognized it. America has also been its ally and supporter. Some Muslim countries that never recognized the State of Israel do not like America friendship with this country. There are moderate Muslim countries that recognize the State of Israel. However, in some of these countries there are extremist groups that hate both the State of Israel and the United States of America despite that America is a secular country with freedom of religion which respects all the countries of the world regardless of their religion.

Some Muslim extremists that have attacked the United States of America say that they will stop attacking this country if America ends its support for the State of Israel; but America will never allow that extremists or terrorists determine its foreign policies.

American Presidents Jimmy Carter, William J. Clinton and George W. Bush have made efforts to achieve peace among the State of Israel and its neighbor countries. The international community has made diplomatic efforts to organize a Palestinian State in the West Bank and in the Gaza Strip that could live in peace with the State of Israel. This is not an easy task, because there are many Palestinians, mainly in the Gaza Strip, that say that the State of Israel does not have right to exist and attack it with suicide bombers and rockets in a continuous way.

At the end of the Second Millennium, the United States of America suffered several attacks from groups belonging to radical "Islamic" movements. These groups said that they attacked the United States of America for the support that this country gives to the State of Israel, and because it has troops in the sacred land of Islam.

These attacks that included a car bomb in the New York City Twin Towers, bombs in two American embassies in Africa, explosion of a boat bomb close to a US Navy war ship in the Arabic peninsula, bombs to installations of American military personnel in Lebanon and Saudi Arabia, and other attacks, were later attributed to Al-Qaeda, a group that said that they were Islamic fighters in a jihad (Holy war), but many Muslims said that they are just extremists and terror-ists and that they can not be called Islamic if they behave that way.

The President William J. Clinton administration gave order to the American military forces to bomb the headquarters of Al-Qaeda in Afghanistan. They were bombed, but it was not clear what was the damage done. Now we know that his leader Osama Bin Laden was not hurt during this attack.

America has now good diplomatic relations with many Muslim countries and with countries in which many people that are Muslim live. In the following paragraphs comments are made in relation to recent conflicts between America and some Muslim countries or extremist groups:

The September Eleven of 2001 Attacks

On September eleven of 2001 the United States of America was attacked. Suicide air pirates took the control of four American jetliners and crashed two of them against the New York City Twin Towers and destroyed them. A third jetliner was crashed against the building of the Department of Defense headquarters in Washington D.C., known as the Pentagon.

A fourth plane crashed in Western Pennsylvania. It is believed that this jetliner was also controlled by air pirates that wanted to crash it against the Nation's Capital, maybe over the White House or the Capitol. However, some plane passengers, who learned of the attacks trough their cellular telephones, did not permit the pirates to continue the flight to Washington D.C. More than three thousand people died in September eleven 2001 attacks.

We know now that the suicide air pirates that attacked the United States of America in September eleven of 2001 were radical Muslims. That most of them were legal immigrants or visitors to the United States of America from Saudi Arabia. They belonged to the organization of Muslim extremists named Al-Qaeda and were trained by this organization for these suicide attacks. Some of them were trained in Afghanistan and others had also lived in Europe before this attack.

The Government of the United States of America learned that the leader of Al-Qaeda was a Muslim extremist named Osama Bin Laden, a citizen of Saudi Arabia who was living in Afghanistan, a country ruled by another extremist group, called the Taliban. Apparently the Taliban did not participate directly in the September 11 attacks, but when the U.S. Government asked for Osama Bin Laden extradition the Taliban said that he was their guest.

The Afhganistan War

After a United Nations resolution, a coalition of countries led by the United States of America made war to Afghanistan with the support of some groups of Afghan revels that were fighting the Taliban Government that ruled that Country.

The coalition forces occupied this Country and a new democratic government under the leadership of Hamid Karzai was established. The Karzai government is stable despite that is attacked frequently by extremists and terrorists who belong to the Taliban and Al-Qaeda.

It is believed that Osama Bin Laden fled to Pakistan. The government of Pakistan is cooperating with The United States of America in the search for Osama Bin Laden, but until September 2008 this government had been unsuccessful in his efforts to find and catch him. There are groups of the Taliban and Al-Qaeda members that hide between Afhganistan and the mountains of the North-West Pakistan area, where it is not easy to catch them. Probably Osama Bin Laden moves continuously with them from one place to another and from one country to another.

The war against Afghanistan was supported by the International Community and by the majority of the people of the United States of America because the Taliban was a partner and the host of the terrorists that attacked the United States of America in September eleven of 2001.

One serious problem that is confronting Afghanistan is the cultivation of "popy" flowers and the production and exportation of illegal drugs obtained from these flowers. For economical reasons the Afghan government efforts to control the cultivation of "popy" flowers have been unsuccessful. It is believed that the terrorists are getting money from the exportation of illegal drugs.

The government of Pakistan is confronting internal political problems that have been complicated after the assassination of the former Prime Minister and opposition leader Benazir Bhutto in the final days of December of 2007. This assassination has been attributed to Al-Qaeda. An investigation about this assassination has been conducted with the support of the British agency Scotland Yard. The stability of Pakistan is very important for the whole world because this country has nuclear weapons. Pakistan has very professional military forces in control of the nuclear weapons, but it would be a disaster if a civil war takes place in this country.

Iraq Occupation of Kuwait

In 1990, Sadam Hussein of Iraq invaded Kuwait another Muslim country that is a member of the United Nations. After Sadam Hussein ignored a mandate from the United Nations to get out of Kuwait or suffer serious consequences, the United Nations attacked Iraq in 1991 with a coalition led by the United States of America.

The Iraq troops were taken out of Kuwait by the United Nations forces. After the war, sanctions were applied to Iraq for its wrongdoing. Before leaving Kuwait, Sadam Hussein burned Kuwait oil wells creating a serious environmental problem and great economical losses.

The War to Finish with Sadam Hussein Regime in Iraq

Sadam Hussein had a war with Iran before the invasion of Kuwait. Sadam Hussein fought against Iran because this country supported groups of Iraq's Shiites that were his enemies. Hussein had used chemical weapons against the Kurd population that live in the North of Iraq. Sadam Hussein was the ruler of a secular regime, but he was a Sunni and he gave very bad treatment to the Iraq's Shiite majority.

Sadam Hussein became an enemy of the United States of America and a suspect of supporting the Al-Qaeda terrorist group. He was also a suspect of making weapons of mass destruction. He was not honoring the United Nations sanctions that had been established against Iraq after his invasion of Kuwait. The war with Iraq is a complicated historical event because this Country never attacked America.

In 2003, the United States of America, the United Kingdom, Spain, Italy and other countries attacked Iraq with a Coalition of Forces that they formed and, after a successful military operation, finished with the dictatorship of Sadam Hussein. Iraq was occupied. The occupation of Iraq was very difficult. Lots of vandalism and of looting happened. Many historic objects disappear from famous museums. The weapons of mass destruction were never found.

Efforts to establish a democratic government have been made. Iraq has now an elected President, a Parliament, a Prime Minister and a Cabinet. But the country has not been stabilized. To establish there a government that can be trusted by everyone is a very difficult mission. Chaos has been created in Iraq by sectarian violence between Shiite and Sunni Muslims a conflict that is more than a millennium old. Attacks from Al-Qaeda also happened every day. Al-Qaeda has also attacked some of the Coalition Forces Countries. In Madrid, Spain, bombs were detonated in the trains system killing many people. The Spanish people voted later to put the ruling party out of office. In England bombs were detonated in the London Metro-rail System with several victims. United Kingdom Prime Minister Tony Blair did not run for reelection.

The President of the United States of America George W. Bush and the Vice-President Cheney together with the former Secretary of Defense Donald Runsfeld were the architects of this war. They told the American people that: (1) it would be a short war. (2) The cost will be moderate. (3) It will stabilize the Middle East. (4) The Americans would be received in Iraq as liberators.

Nothing of that happened. More than 4,000 Americans have been killed in this war. The cost of this war is over one trillion dollars. The dollar of the United States of America became very weak after this war. The approval rating of President George W. Bush became below 30%.

For different reasons the occupation of Iraq has been a disaster. The sponsors of this war thought that this was going to be a small conflict. They underestimated the consequences of this war in the future stabilities of Iraq and the neighbor country Pakistan; and overestimated the capacity of the United States of America to handle this conflict. They never thought that this war would become almost like another Vietnam War. They thought that this war was going to be like the previous war against Iraq that was called Desert Storm or First Iraq War in which the American casualties were limited.

After a successful military operation, the American troops, that won the war easily, are now policing the country in the middle of a sectarian violence, a job for which they were not originally trained. Most of the American casualties have occurred after the occupation.

The President George W. Bush administration says that the Iraq war is part of a general war against international terrorists and Al-Qaeda, but many people believe that Al-Qaeda was not a partner of Saddam Hussein and that Al-Qaeda went to fight in Iraq only after its occupation by the United States of America and the Coalition Forces.

Complications of the Iraq War

The war in Iraq constitutes a complicated historical situation for several reasons:

a) The United States of America, a country that was born fighting for freedom, and against an empire, now occupies Iraq and its strongest allied in this effort is precisely the United Kingdom, the country that had occupied Iraq in 1920, and had established the biggest empire that ever existed in the World. It is very difficult for the Iraqi people to believe that the United States of America and the United Kingdom are there because they want to help them. They would prefer that they leave Iraq.

b) Not everyone that fights against a foreign power that is occupying his country is necessarily a terrorist. Some Iraqis united the war against the Coalition Forces, just because they are occupiers. Other Iraqis fight the Coalition Forces because they believe that they are allays of their enemies in the sectarian war they have between themselves.

c) The occupying powers do not know how to settle the more than a millennium old conflict between Shiites and Sunnis.

d) A war with imperialistic characteristics is an anachronism in this Third Millennium.

e) Most Europeans do not like the occupation of Iraq because it remembers them the preemptive and aggressive wars of Napoleon Bonaparte and Adolfo Hitler that were a disaster for Europe and for the World. To occupy a country is a dangerous decision. Aggressors know how to initiate wars but they never know what will be their evolution and how they will finish. Sometimes they are successful at the beginning but in the long term they lose.

f) The Iraq war has weakened the capacity of the United States of America to deal with other problems, including the situation in other parts of the Middle East and with internal problems like the natural disasters, etc.

g) The aggressive interrogation policies and abuse of prisoners in Abu Ghraib has deteriorated the image of the United States of America as a civilized country that respect human rights and the Geneva Convention.

Ideas in order that American Troops Get out of the Muslim Countries

The American People and the People of Iraq want that the United States of America leave Iraq. But the United States of America and the Coalition Forces cannot leave that Country in the chaotic state it is in the year 2008. The best choice is to help the elected Iraqi Government to establish control over the Country before leaving it. As soon as the Iraqi Government become able to manage that Country by itself, it will be convenient that the United States of America Forces and the other Coalition Forces leave the Country gradually.

It is not easy to have a strong democratic Government in Iraq. It is not easy to have a Prime Minister accepted and trusted by all the Iraqi ethnic groups. But the Iraqis have to understand that their only way to get peace and stability is to learn to live together with respect to peoples who are different, think different or worship different.

We have to understand that there are groups like the Taliban and Al-Qaeda that do not want the Iraqi, Afghan and

Pakistani governments to succeed. They do not want a world in peace where the Muslim Countries have friendly relations with the West. They want a total confrontation of cultures and religions. They think that the people that do not believe like they believe are infidels that have not right to exist.

It is necessary that the Muslim countries control the extremist and terrorist groups in their territories by themselves, without the presence of foreign troops in order to have a better and safer world. The presence of foreign troops in Muslim countries is unhelpful because it transforms the fanatics and terrorists in nationalist heroes.

In order to have a peaceful and more stable world it is necessary that the Muslim Countries, the Western Countries, and the rest of the countries of the world, work together with the purpose of having a better knowledge of their cultures, their religions and their values.

It is very important in the globalize world of the future that all people around the world have respect for all religions and for the liberty of conscience of people everywhere.

America and Iran Relations

America, together with other countries supported Iran in the development of its oil resources and became a good customer of Iran oil exports for many years. During the years of the1950s and 1960s the relations between the governments of Iran and the United States of America were very friendly. However during the 1970s the government of the Shah Mohammad Reza Pahlavi confronted opposition from a movement that wanted to establish an Islamic Republic. This movement did not like the United States of America for the support that it was giving to the Iran Shah Regime and to the State of Israel.

In January 1979 the Shah government was defeated and the Iran Islamic Republic was established. The Ayatollah Ruhollah Khomeini became the leader of the new Islamic Republic. In October 1979, with the support of the Ayatollah Khomeini Iranian students took hostage 66 persons in the American Embassy in Teheran. The hostages were freed in January 1981 after the inauguration of President Ronald Reagan. Since October 1979 there are not diplomatic relations between the Islamic Republic of Iran and the United States of America.

In 2008 the United States of America continue without diplomatic relations with Iran. It is believed that Iran has been making efforts to get nuclear weapons. However, it looks that after the wars in Afhganistan and Iraq it decided to stop the nuclear weapons program. Apparently, Iran has continued enriching uranium only to get fuel for a nuclear power plant that is being built there.

Iran supports the enemies of Israel in Lebanon and Palestine who attack frequently Israel with rockets. Iran has been accused of sending weapons to the terrorists that attack the American troops in Iraq.

The problem with Iran is very complicated for the United Nations because the President of this Country, that is a member of the United Nations, has said that the State of Israel, another member of the United Nations, has to be wiped out of the map of the Middle East.

4 The Economic Recession

For people who are not economist or financial specialists, it was very difficult to understand the message of President George W. Bush, that he would reduce taxes and at the same time he would have enough money to fight the war against Saddam Hussein and the extremists and terrorists in Iraq and elsewhere. He said that the hard earn money that people made is for them, no to pay taxes to the government of the United States of America. That sounds fine, but President Bush administration has spent more than two trillion dollars in the American military forces, the Iraq and other wars at the same time that he has been reducing taxes; if the Americans are not paying for these military expenses and for these wars, who is paying for them?

In mathematics there is a concept called "reduction to the absurd" that helps to explain this matter: If a government charges no taxes to people, the government has no money and becomes broken. If a government charges very high taxes the people have no money and the economy becomes broken. After the economy becomes broken the government also becomes broken.

The taxes can be adjusted to such a level that stimulates the economy, which becomes stronger, and the government collects more money. There is a point that can be called the optimum tax rate whish is not easy to know specially to politicians in congress. When politicians, demagogues or economists talk about tax reductions, what they are talking about is tax rate adjustments, in order to stimulate the economy, increase production and get more money from the people.

However, taxes can be gotten from the big corporations and the rich people, and from the middle class and from the working people. If the government establishes very high taxes for the big corporations and for the rich people, they do not invest in business and the economy does not grow. On the other hand, if the government establishes very high taxes to the middle class and the working people, they do not have money to buy goods, to buy new cars, to buy new homes, etc., and the economy goes down. The establishment of tax rates is not a science, it is an art and it is very difficult. It is complicated by the fact that big corporations spend lots of money lobbying congressmen in order that they pass laws favorable for the corporations. The middle class and the working class cannot spend the same amounts of money lobbying congressmen, but they have the power of the vote in elections. This is why good and honest leadership is so important in democratic countries.

The trillions of dollars spent in the military and in the wars went out of the general economy; they went to the military people, to the military contractors, to the weapons and munition factories, and to the contractors for the reconstruction of the destroyed countries. But these billions of dollars went out of many sectors of the economy that are weaker now. The economy would have been better if this money would have been invested in new plants and equipment, in education and in welfare. With the billions spent in these wars all the transportation infrastructure of the United States of America could have been fixed and renewed where it is necessary.

We can say that there is not limit to the price we have to pay to secure America. But America could have been secured in a better way without losing the lives of thousands of American soldiers and billions of dollars in Iraq. After this war the capacity of the United States of America to fight the extremists and terrorists that hate and want to attack America has been diminished.

President George W. Bush says that we will prevail in Iraq, but it is not clear what that means. A peaceful and stable Iraq with friendly relations with America can be accepted as a victory, but if that happens after the high cost that this war have had for America, it would be similar to the victory of the Greek King Pyrrhus over the Romans in 280 B.C.

Of course, if the construction companies and the oil companies go to Iraq after the "victory" they will make profits, but these profits will not compensate for the sacrifice that the American people and the American military have made, and for the billions of dollars wasted there. In his last State of the Union address to Congress, in January 2008, President George W. Bush said that the United States of America will prevail in Iraq and will secure its presence in the Persian Gulf. This affirmation is an imperialistic anachronism typical of the old oil companies and of the days of Manifest Destiny. In relation to today's world demand for oil, the Persian Gulf oil reserves are not so important to deserve this dramatic deterioration of the American economy. These oil reserves will be spent in a few decades, and if we believe in freedom, we have to accept that the countries that export oil are free to sell their oil to the countries they want.

The higher prices in fuels that the increase in consumption and the war has originated represent a cost higher than all the tax reductions made. The money has gone to the oil companies who are very happy for a while. But at the end they and the community will suffer the same final problem that suffers a government that charges very high taxes: the economy is weaker, the dollar is weaker, unemployment is higher, and people cannot pay their house mortgage and their debts. People do not buy new automobiles. The construction industry is paralyzed because the houses cannot be sold. In the first months of 2008 the stock market lost more than all the gains made in 2007.

If we take into consideration the lower value of the dollar, and also the losses in the value of the stocks in dollars, we have to accept that in the year 2008 the losses have been very dramatic and that we are in the beginning of a RECESSION; however the most pessimistic forecasters say that we are in the beginning of a DEPRESSION. But what is the difference between a recession and a depression? A depression is a very strong recession. A moderate negative economic growth longer than six months can be identify as a recession, and a dramatic negative economic growth longer than a year can be identify as a depression. There is a famous comment of President Harry Truman about this issue. He said that "we are in recession when our neighbors lose their jobs, and we are in depression when we lose our jobs."

The high economic growth of the Asian countries at the beginning of the third millennium, including China and India, has made the oil reserves of the world small in relation to the demand, and the price of oil will increase in a continuous way. As the oil reserves become smaller the prices of oil will go higher. The whole world will suffer a great depression because the scarcity of fuels and its high price will stop the economic growth worldwide; and this will be sooner than we believe. The best way to minimize this world disaster is to construct more nuclear power plants and to increase the volume of public transportation powered by electricity. Individual transportation in automobiles will have to be limited for short distances. It will be also important to develop the hydraulic and geothermic resources available worldwide. We have created a civilization that needs great amounts of energy, and we cannot stop it because the oil reserves are over. France is a country prepared better than the United States of America for this new situation. France generates eighty per cent of its electricity from nuclear power, and it has a good network of modern electric trains.

In addition to the billions of dollars spent in Iraq, there are other factors that have stimulated the 2008 recession: a) the high cost of healthcare and prescription drugs; b) the high cost of higher education c) the high cost of housing; d) the high cost of gasoline and fuels, e) the growing debt of the United States of America and the payment of its interests, e) the dramatic loss of value of the American dollar, f) the natural disasters, including the Katrina hurricane in New Orleans, and g) the return to their original countries of many immigrants, for the lack of jobs in construction and other activities, leaving their houses abandoned and ready for fore-closure. Some immigrants are also leaving the United States of America for the unfriendly attitude of some American toward the immigrants, including some local governments and some television commentators. Many farmers are hav-ing problems recruiting the labor force they need to harvest their farm's products.

Special comment deserves the weakening of the American dollar. Traditionally the dollar of the United States of America was considered as the world currency and America had the capacity to make emissions of dollars freely, with-out an important currency to establish a comparison. The European Euro has changed everything. Today we can see everyday how the U.S. dollar becomes weaker than the Euro.

Everyday more countries and companies want to have their reserves in Euros. It looks like a joke, but at the end of 2007 a Brazilian model girl that was invited to come to work in the United States of America said that she would come only if the contract was made with the payments in Euros.

The increase in the number of home mortgage foreclosures is a cause of concern. The people that signed mortgage loans and lost their jobs, the immigrants that left the United States of America and had no time to sale their homes, the people that made loans without a fix interest rate, and others that can not get along with the increasing cost of life are losing their homes. The banks are taking the houses, but cannot sell them quickly. The empty homes are invaded and destroyed by crooks and illegal drug addicts, or infested by mice, roaches, termites and other insects. The banks do not know what to do, because they were designed to finance people, not to administrate empty homes or to spend their money securing empty homes. Because of these problems, the stocks of many banks that finance mortgages are going down in value.

Traditionally one of the symptoms of recession was the lack of economic growth. Economists assume that economic growth is parallel to good quality of life. But the world is now close to an age that will be called the post-economic age, in which the environmental dimension is becoming more important than economic growth.

The environmental dimension has been important always, but it has not been considered correctly in the past. The economic feasibility studies that demonstrated a good Benefit Cost ratio for the oil extraction in the Amazon jungles of Ecuador and Peru, did not take into consideration the negative change in the quality of life and the fate of the Native Americans that live there and have been there for millenniums. The modern economists were no different from the Spanish, English, French and Portuguese "conquistadores" that came to America in the XVI century; the economist's main concern was the rate of return that the investors would receive. Only in the last decades, the development banks started asking to loan applicants for environmental impact studies of their development projects.

Today the environmental problem is not only for the local people of a developing area. It is a problem for mankind. We are talking about the global warming, and about the survival of planet Earth. India, China, and many other countries are making efforts to emulate the level of development reached by America, Europe and some South-East Asian countries. If the whole world reaches this level of development, and they have the right to try to reach it, the world consumption of energy will arrive to levels never imagined, the global warming will go faster, and the reserves of fossil fuels and other resources will last shorter than ever thought. We are close to the point in historic times, when economic growth will no longer mean necessarily a better quality of life but the reverse.

The word recession has a new meaning. In one hand it means that all the traditional problems of the past recessions will be present, including great amounts of people without jobs and the very serious consequences of the situation. On the other hand, recession now means a reduction in the environmental impact of intensive development, which is good.

A long recession or depression will be the process through which the development path of the last hundred years will change. However, if this change is not oriented in a civilized and smart way many millions of people will suffer.

In accordance to United Nation estimations, at the beginning of the third millennium, the population of the Earth has grown to 6.0 billion of persons. In 1960, the Earth's population was 3.0 billion. In 1900, the population was 1.65 billion; and in the year 1 AD the population was 300 millions. It is estimated that in the year 2050 the Earth's population will reach 9.0 billion. It took 1600 years to growth from 300 million to 3.0 billion; but it took only 40 years to growth from 3.0 billion to 6.0 billion. This extraordinary growth is attributed to the industrial revolution and to the advances in sanitation, health care and medicine.

For planet Earth it is not the same thing to feed 3.0 billion people (1960) than 9.0 billion (2050). The area of forests that have to be destroyed and transformed in agricultural lands will be three times bigger. The destruction of the forests will originate higher water levels in the rivers and more floods during the rainy seasons, and lower water flows and scarcity of water during the dry seasons. The quality of the water will be deteriorated for the use of more agrochemicals and for the increase in wastes disposal. The energy consumption will be also three times bigger unless a change in energy consumption happens. The oil and other fossil fuels will be almost exhausted, and the civilization could survive only with the use of nuclear power and other new sources of energy.

We can see the environmental deterioration that occurred between 1960 and 2000 with 3.0 billion additional persons. It is difficult to see in advance what will happen in 2050 with another additional 3.0 billion persons, if all reach today's level of development in Europe, America and the South East of Asia. It is better not to imagine what would be planet Earth in the year 3000 if the present rate of population and economic growth continues everywhere. It is obvious that a new approach for population growth, consumption of energy, and consumption of the Earth resources is required.

At present population growth is controlled mainly in the rich developed countries, which have a tendency to have an old population, do not get internally all the labor force they need, and receive many immigrants. On the other hand, the poor underdeveloped countries do not control population growth, the population is very young, and they do not have enough jobs for everyone. This pattern of population control is not working well. Many problems are presented for the way in which it is happening. Many people from the poor countries migrate to the rich countries looking for jobs; however not all the people of the poor countries that need jobs can be received by the developed countries.

We read documents telling us that Native Americans and Indigenous people in many parts of the world were masters in conservation and protection of the natural resources and of the environment. This is true, and we can learn many things from them. But we cannot feed the billions of people of today's world with their production technologies. Many of the social problems and lack of peace between different communities that we see today in Africa and other parts of the world are related to great populations and limited production and inadequate conservation, storage and distribution of food which originate food supply crisis, especially after long droughts.

The best approach to solve the problems that will be presented in this difficult new world is a gradual change of attitude.

We have to learn that the western model of civilization with its high consumption of the world resources has to change for a more frugal life; it has to make many changes, including a reduction in consumption, more savings, less luxuries, less unnecessary traveling, looking for happiness trough spiritual values and not only through money and material goods. We need to take advantage of the computer age that allows us to many things, including to work without traveling every day to the work place, to make payments without going to the lender's offices, etc. The collective public transportation has to be increased, and the private transportation has to be decreased. In general, all the comments made in others parts of this book about the reduction of the consumption of energy and about the use of alternative sources of energy have to be followed as soon as possible.

However many of the projects proposed recently to stimulate the economy have to be carried out because the change have to be gradual in order to limit the pain and human suffering that this changing situation could cause. In the United States of America, where the unemployment rate had increased in 2008, the government is sending to tax payers rebate checks to stimulate the economy. In Venezuela, petrodollars rich President Hugo Chaves government is sending checks to the poor and unemployed people to help them in their difficult situation, to stimulate the economy and to reduce crime, because honest people without money to buy food for their children have to get it anyway.

One interesting aspect of the new recession in the United States of America is that people will stop migrating to the United States of America and will start going back to their original countries, because the lack of jobs will make the United States of America unattractive for new immigrants.

The people who do not like the arrival of new immigrants to America at least should be happy for this aspect of the recession. It is possible that many Americans will start migrating to other countries were they can have a better quality of life with their savings, and pensions as is happening with the migration of senior Americans to Costa Rica and other countries of Latin America.

5. The Barack Obama Phenomenon

Hawaii became one state of the United States of America in August 21, 1959. Barack Obama was born in Honolulu, Hawaii in August 4, 1961. He was the child of the marriage of a white American woman from Kansas with an African Student from Kenya; as a child he went to school in Hawaii and Indonesia where he attended a catholic school and a secular school where many students were muslim; but he never was a member of those religions.

After Barack Obama graduated from Harvard Law School, he decided to work for the people and not for the corporations. He was more interested in people than in money, and he wanted to help people. He initiated his work as a community organizer and a civil rights attorney. Easily he became a leader in the fight against unemployment and poverty in the city of Chicago, Illinois. Barack Obama worked with organizations that were helping workers who lost their jobs to modify their work profile and adjust to labor changing situations.

The work of Barack Obama became popular and known to the people of Chicago who elected him to the Illinois Congress, where he served as a State Senator from 1997 to 2004. In 2000 Barack Obama fail an effort to become a member of the United States House of Representatives, but later he was elected a United States Senator from Illinois, where he has served since January 4, 2005.

Barack Obama always felt the presence of God. But he was exposed to different cultures in different countries and he saw different ways of worship. He married a Christian woman and decided to become a Christian and to be the head of a Christian family.

Barack Obama attended the Trinity United Church of Christ in Chicago, who's Pastor, a man with the name Jeremiah Wright, had some beliefs and manner of preaching that sound wrong to many Americans. For example, he did not ask "God to bless America, but to damn America" for what was happening in this country to many black people. Some enemies of Barack Obama tried to "assassinate his character" saying that Pastor Wright was his mentor, and that Obama had the same ideas and the same thinking of Pastor Wright. But Barack Obama made a bright presentation demonstrating that his philosophy, his message and his feelings were quite different from those of Pastor Wright, despite that he was a member of his church and that Jeremiah Wright had been the pastor who married him and his wife Michelle and baptized their two daughters.

In 2008 the Senator Barack Obama won the Presidential Primary elections of the Democratic Party of the United States of America. A movement led by college students, union leaders and common people finally chose Barack Obama as the Democratic candidate for President of the United States of America. Finally, there is a chance that the government of the corporations, by the corporations, for the corporations becomes again the "government of the people, by the people for the people." However, Barack Obama and the people who chose him do not believe that the corporations are over. They are friendly to the corporations and they believe that they are and they will continue being very important and necessary. The Americans know very well that the corporations create products, goods, and services for the people, and more important, the corporations create jobs for the people, and the people cannot survive without jobs. The issue here is that the people do not exist to work for the corporations. The corporations exist to work for the people. Like in any democracy, the government of the United States of America must represent the will of the people.

The important issue is the social responsibility of capital. The weapons industry exist not to make a big business but to protect America and to defend democracy and the security of the people. The pharmaceutical companies do not exist to make big business with sky level price products, but to produce pharmaceutical products to cure the people at reasonable prices. The oil companies exist to facilitate transportation, not to make big business in a speculative market. Of course, they have to make profits, because if they do not make profits they disappear, and we need them.

For the first time in History a person with African background has a chance to become the most important leader of the most powerful country in the world. It happens just a few decades after the times when in America the black people had to travel in the back seats of the buses, and less than two centuries after it was a crime in America to teach black people how to read or how to write.

Many people in America and in the World thought that Barack Obama could not be elected President because he was an African American, and there are many white people, especially old white people in some parts of the America, who would not vote for him just because he is a black man. But there was also a symmetric balance, many African Americans who traditionally did not vote in national elections, because they saw them as a business of white people, were ready this time to vote for Barack Obama.

Young Americans of all races and backgrounds support Barack Obama because they are inspired by his messages about the need for change and peace that could be compared in quality and strength with the messages of John F. Kennedy and Martin Luther King.

The election of Barack Obama would be important not only for America, but for the whole World. Many of the so-called Third World Countries, which saw the United States of America as a continuation of the European imperialism, are surprised to see a black man leading in this country. However, the true is that America was born as a country fighting imperialism, and America is a country that fought a big war to end with slavery.

The Barack Obama democratic government program is offering to the world a foreign policy in which the United States of America would be again a big power helping the international community to fight aggression worldwide. The recent American policies of unilateral pre-emptive wars would finish in the Barack Obama democratic administration. The World would be more peaceful and a better place to live.

The candidate of the Republican Party, Senator John McCain, is a good one. John McCain is a good person, a good American and a patriot. He fought in the Vietnam War, and was a war prisoner there for more than five years.

John McCain was born in Panama, in the Canal Zone, in 1936 where his grand father, a U.S. Navy Admiral, was the American Chief Executive Officer of the Panama Canal Zone; and his father, another U.S. Navy Admiral, was the Captain of an U.S. Navy ship. *See Related Story 5: The Panama Canal.*

John McCain graduated from the U.S. Naval Academy in Annapolis, MD, and served in the U.S. Navy from 1958 to 1981. In 1982 he was elected to represent Arizona in the U.S. House of Representatives; and since 1986 he has been a U.S. Senator for Arizona.

John McCain talks all the time about the necessity to reduce expenses; but he supports the Bush Iraq war and the idea that the United States of America military has to be present in the Persian Gulf, whatever its cost, because there is too much oil in this area. But this policy is imperialistic, has originated too much suffering to America and Iraq, broken the American and the World economies, and constitutes an anachronism in the year 2008. The United States of America was born fighting for freedom and against an empire, not to become another empire.

The year 2008 was a special one. A woman, Nancy Pelosi, was the Speaker of the House of Representatives for the first time in the History of America. Another woman, Hilary Clinton almost becomes for the first time the candidate of the Democratic Party to the Presidency of the United States of America. Condolezza Rice is the first African American woman to be National Security Advisor and Secretary of State. The concept that America has to be led only by white males is finally over.

Barack Obama is not just a black leader. He is an American Leader who inspired the American people of all races and backgrounds and convinced them that something can be done to solve the energy crisis, the immigration crisis, the economic crisis, and to change the foreign policy path that the country has followed in the first eight years of the Third Millennium.

The Obama movement demonstrated that there are new technologies that offer new ways to communicate with people and that the expensive traditional media is no longer the only way. The Obama movement demonstrated also that millions of people donating small contributions could be more powerful than groups of powerful industries and corporations supporting a political campaign.

After the Iraq war fiasco and its catastrophic economical consequences for America and the World, the people wanted a change, and the Obama movement represented a change. The Obama movement has offered to end the American occupation of Iraq as soon as possible but in a safe and wise way. A mistake has been made, but now we have to manage the situation carefully.

It is obvious that the World cannot continue its dependency from the oil producing countries because this dependency has become a source of instability and have weakened the independence and self-determination of the countries that have to import oil. The Obama movement has indicated that the solution of the energy crisis in a holistic way is one of their priorities.

The Obama movement has offered a human approach to the migration crisis, taking into consideration the safety of America, the security of our borders, but also the human rights of people that have spent many years working in America undocumented, and that have been living here because America has allowed them to stay here because we need them.

The Obama movement has also recognized that the difficult economic situation that we have in America today has to be solved through leadership giving confidence to the investors and entrepreneurs that have to develop many activities in order to recover the economy and the energetic independency of America. These activities will require great capital amounts and will generate many new jobs for the American People.

The Obama movement recognizes that the solution to the energy crisis cannot be found occupying oil rich countries like Iraq, but developing new energy sources in America.

America, the country of freedom, has to recognize that the countries rich in oil resources are free to sell their oil to the countries they want at the price they can get. In order to avoid energetic vulnerability, America has to develop its own energy sources and end its dependency in imported oil.

America has to get the power to stop doing business with arrogant leaders of countries rich in oil resources. America has to get the power to stop doing business and sending money to countries that do not like us or hate us.

During the Second World War Franklin Delano Roosevelt saved the World transforming the American civil industry into a military industry creating what he called "the arsenal of democracy."

At the beginning of the Third Millenium the Barack Obama movement can save the World if it convinces the Military Industry, the Oil Industry and all the other American industrialists and entrepreneurs that they have to support the efforts to create the new energy sources of democracy.

A Barack Obama government would start its activities under a serious economic depression. There are many house fore-closures, there is a high inflation, and most Americans know that the money they earn is not enough to pay for the cost of food, for the cost of housing, for other costs of living; for the education of their children, for the healthcare expenses, etc. Today many Americans are solvent until they get sick.

An economic reactivation plan has to be developed. The look for new sources of energy can help in the economic reactivation creating new jobs and reducing the costs of energy. Something has to be done to reduce the high prices of prescription drugs.

The financial system has to end with speculative interest rates in credit cards and other financial services. Efforts have to be made to facilitate higher education to the children of middle and lower class families. More scholarships at all levels of education have to be offered to the children of all economic levels that are outstanding students.

Under a Barack Obama government, all the Americans would know that the opportunities that the country offers to them are limitless independently of their race, national origin, or background. The skills, the capacity and the knowledge of the people would define the levels at which they could offer their services to the community.

SECOND PART: HISTORICAL ROOTS

6 Origins of the United States of America and Mexico Migration Situation

The Population of Mexico

In 1519 when Hernan Cortes and the Spanish conquerors of Mexico saw for the first time the City of Tenochtitlan, the Capital of the Aztec Empire, they were surprised of its size, because in those days it was bigger than any city they had seen in Europe before. At that time the Aztec Empire was at his highest point. Tenochtitlan had many canals and the Spaniards called it the Venice of the new world. This city, built over a lake, was in the same place where today is Mexico City, the Capital of Mexico, a big city and one of the most beautiful capitals of the world.

When the Muslims intended to occupy Europe in the VII Century, Spain stopped them. It is possible that Spain and the East European Countries saved what today is known as the Western Culture or Western Civilization. But after eight centuries of war against the Muslim occupiers, Spain became a country with only one religion, the Roman Catholic. The Kings Ferdinand and Elizabeth, the sponsors of Columbus voyages, were known as the Catholic Kings of Spain.

Under these rulers the people that did not follow the Catholic Church doctrine and commandments were considered heretic. The heretics were taken out of Spain or punished. Many of the heretics were victims of the merciless Spanish Inquisition. It was a common practice to take the property and goods of wealthy people accusing them of being heretic. Spain continued with this policy of only one religion in Mexico and all the Spanish Empire. The Catholic Church organization was a very important instrument in the management of the Spanish Empire.

After the arrival of the Spaniards, many Native Americans died of diseases for which they did not have immunity, that were brought to these continents by the Europeans. It is possible that were brought Native Americans died victim of these diseases than as victims of the wars with the conquerors. At the same time, many diseases, that did not exist in Europe before, were brought by the Europeans to Europe when they went back there.

Mexico is a beautiful country that attracts many tourists from the whole World. Its mariachis, its music and its dances that reunited Spanish and Native American culture are very good; a good place to see them are the Fine Arts Palace and the Plaza Garibaldi in Mexico City. The beaches of Acapulco, Cancun, and the Island of Cozumel are important tourist attractions.

The pyramids of Teotihuacan, near Mexico City, other Aztec's archeological places and the Maya's archeological places in Merida, Yucatan are visited and admired by archeologists and tourists.

Despite that the Spaniards said that the main objective of the conquest of the Americas was to convert the Native Americans to the Christian religion, many Native American men were slaved and sent to work in the mines and agricultural fields. Some Spanish priests, like Fray Bartolome de las

Casas, protested for the bad treatment given to the Native Americans in the Spanish colonies.

Many Native American women had children with Spaniards giving origin to the "Mestizos" or Spanish-Native American people who constitute today a high percentage of the population in some countries of Latin America. There are many communities where the Native Americans did not mix with Europeans, or mixed with them only a little. It is estimated that in Mexico there are almost ten million of Native Americans. This is close to ten percent of the total population.

The extension of the Maya Country included the South of Mexico, Guatemala, Honduras, Belize and El Salvador. A high percentage of the population that live close to the border between Mexico and Guatemala are Maya descendants. Some of these groups had been recently upset and disappointed because in different opportunities they had been persecuted or harassed by military personnel from these countries that had been looking for terrorists or revolutionaries.

The North America Free Trade Agreement (NAFTA) and the Reaction of the Zapatist Rebels.

The trade agreements between the United States of America and Canada have worked fluid for many years. Recently Mexico was included in the North America Free Trade Agreement called NAFTA. The Government of Mexico and some sectors of this Country were happy with the NAFTA. They said that now the Mexican industries will have better markets, and that it will be easier to get many needed materials, industrial equipment and parts. But in the other hand many peasants most of them Native Americans said that they could not survive with this agreement. Some of their leaders were disappointed. They said that now the potatoes produced in Idaho and the corn produced in the Midwest of the United States of America will be cheaper in Mexico than the crops that they produce in Chiapas.

NAFTA became a market of three countries with more than four hundred million people. It is an important one. Many South and Central American Countries have joined it or want to join it.

In January 1, 1994 the NAFTA became effective. It was the same day that the Subcomandante Marcos and his Zapatist Rebels attacked several towns in the Mexican State of Chiapas and took them. The Mexican Federal Government sent troops to Chiapas. Monseñor Samuel Ruiz, the Catholic Bishop of San Cristobal de las Casas, Chiapas, offered his services as a mediator. He knew some of the Zapatists and wanted to avoid a confrontation between them and the Mexican Federal Troops. The Government accepted the offer of the Bishop and sent negotiators to Chiapas.

Despite the Bishop efforts, some fights occurred between the Zapatists and the Government troops, and more than one hundred persons died. Later the Zapatists abandoned the towns and fled to the jungle. Many Native Americans took refuge in the Catholic Churches, and some of them were burned. But the negotiations between the Government and the Zapatists were initiated. The Zapatist Rebels said that they belonged to the Ejercito Zapatista de Liberacion Nacional (EZLN), or Zapatist National Liberation Army.

The Zapatists got their names from Emiliano Zapata a revolutionary leader that was assassinated in 1919 after many years of struggle in support of the rights of the peasants and Native Americans.

The Zapatists were angry with Mexico's ruling Political Party the PRI (Institutional Revolutionary Party.) They said that after more than sixty five years of only that party in the Government of Mexico, only the rights of the rich and the corporations were protected, and that the poor are having difficulties to survive and their rights are not respected. They gave a document to the Government negotiators indicating what their demands were. Among their petitions there were demands for better distribution of the land. More land have to be given to the Native Americans. The Government negotiators told that they had to go back to Mexico City to consider the Zapatists' demands with other Government Officials. But the parts agree to a cease-fire. It was not an easy negotiation. Enough time was needed to consider, discuss and negotiate the Zapatists' demands.

At the end of 1994 the Zapatists withdrew from the negotiations when they saw that the Government was sending more troops to the area. They attacked and took more towns but the Government fought them and they fled again to the jungle. The Government decided to create a National Negotiation Commission to consider the issues demanded by the Zapatists. The members of this Commission reinitiated talks with the Zapatists.

In 1995 The New President of Mexico Ernesto Zedillo ordered to the federal troops in Chiapas to take some towns that the Zapatists were controlling again. Later President

Zedillo Government and the Zapatists agree to another cease-fire, and the negotiations continued.

In January 1996 the Zapatists agree to become a civil and political movement. They changed their name to Frente Zapatista de Liberacion Nacional (FZLN) or Zapatist National Liberation Front. The Mexican Government made efforts to honor the agreements that have been negotiated. New legislation was passed that facilitated the participation of the FZLN in the political process. And measures were taken to minimize the negative effects of NAFTA in the economy and agriculture of Chiapas.

The area of Mexico where the Zapatists are is one of the poorest in the Country. There are in this part of the Country social problems, health problems and economic problems. These problems are not all new. Most of them are not related to NAFTA, but the Zapatists believe that NAFTA will deteriorate the situation.

In the year 2000 for the first time in seventy years the Institutional Revolutionary Party lost the elections in Mexico. A new President, Vicente Fox was elected. He took the federal troops out of Chiapas. The Zapatists are now a political movement, not an army.

Many Mexicans said that in the last decades they had not a dictator, but that they had the dictatorship of only one political party.

Good questions for the Mexican political analysts are:

Who finish with the roll of the Institutional Revolutionary Party (PRI) as "one party dictatorship in Mexico"?

The Zapatistas.?

The NAFTA?

The people of Mexico tired of so many years with the PRI in power?

The advances in communications, like the e-mails, the Internet or the cellular telephones?

The difficult economic situation and lack of good jobs, which are considered as factors that have stimulated the migration of Mexicans to the United States of America?

The Population of the United States of America

The Native Americans that lived at the arrival of the Europeans in the territory that today belongs to the United States of America did not have great cities, like Mexico's Tenochtitlan or great empires like the Incas or the Aztecs. But there were many Native American Countries in North America. Sometimes they had wars with neighbors, but they were very free people, never conquered by a big empire. They had a tradition of respect for their ancestors and old people. They were lovers of Nature and made a wise use of natural resources.

Since the beginning of the conquest and colonization the original United States of America was populated by European people of different religions looking for freedom of conscience and worship.

The English colonization brought families to America. At the beginning some of the colonists had friendly encounters with Native Americans, but at the end they became enemies. The colonists had many wars with the Natives killing them and destroying the towns and villages where they lived.

What we can see today is that in the United States of America exist a limited number of Native Americans, in relation to the total population. The Navajo, the most populous Indian group in the United States of America, has today a population of almost 100,000 persons. Some of the Native Americans live in "reservations." It is not easy to find in the United States of America people whose origin is from a mixture of Native Americans and Europeans, with the exception, of course, of the people that belonged before to Mexico and other countries of Latin America.

In the United States of America there have been several waves of immigrants from England, Ireland, Germany, Holland, Poland, Italy, Russia, Greece, the Scandinavian and other European countries. There have been waves of immigrants from China, India, Japan, Korea, Vietnam and other Asian countries.

The immigration from Africa requires special consideration because before the end of the nineteenth century the Africans did not come to America by their own will. They came slaved by the Europeans and by the Americans. The problem of slavery is considered later in this book in the part about the American Civil War.

Expansion of the Territory of the United States of America

The territory of the United States of America grew rapidly. In the year 1803 it almost doubled its territory through the Louisiana Purchase from France. In 1813 it acquired Florida by treaty with Spain. In 1845 it was the Texas Annexation. In 1846 the United States of America received the Oregon country after it signed a treaty with England.

In 1848 there was a war between the United States of America and Mexico. After that war, Mexico, that had lost Texas three year earlier, lost another important part of its territory. In 1868 The United States of America acquired Alaska from Russia.

The Latin American neighbors and the rest of the world became nervous for the rapid expansion of the United States of America that had become a Giant. The Government of this Country understood that, and the process did not continue until the war with Spain at the end of the Nineteenth Century. After that it stopped, with the only exception of the acquisition of the territory necessary for the Panama Canal, which after eighty years of operation of the Canal was given back to Panama.

But there were American adventurers, called Filibusters, like the infamous William Walker, that wanted that the territorial expansion of the United States of America continued, and went to Mexico and Central America with that purpose. *See Related Story 4: William Walker* in the Third Part of this book. *See Related Story 5: the Panama Canal* in the Third Part of this book.

Analysis of Some Demographic Aspects of Mexico and the United States of America

The ruins of the Maya civilization found in Central America and Mexico, and the dimension of the Aztec Empire found in Mexico at the arrival of the Spaniards gives us the idea that in the Sixteenth Century the Native American population of today Mexico was much larger than the Native American population in what today is the territory of the United States of America. This is one of the reasons why Mexico has a bigger Native American and "Mestizo" population than the United States of America.

From 1984 to 2006, the population of Mexico, a country of 758 thousands of square miles grew from 76.8 to 107.4 millions of inhabitants. In the same period, the population of the United States of America, a Country of 3,794 thousands of square miles the population grew from 236.3 to 298.4 millions of inhabitants. This means that in this period the population density Mexico increased in 40.4 inhabitants per square mile (from 101.3 to 141.7,) while the population density of the United States of America increased in 16.4 inhabitants per square mile (from 62.3 to 78.7.) Other way to analyze this data is to say that in that last period of 22 years the population of Mexico grew 39.8% while the population of the United States of America grew 26.3 %.

If we assume that in the same period ten million of Mexicans that migrated from Mexico to the United States of America did not do that, the population's densities increases would be: 53.56 inhabitants per square mile in Mexico, and 13.73 inhabitants per square mile in the United States of America. That means that the increase of the population density of

Mexico in that period is almost four times that of the United States of America. That means also that without the migration that happens the increase of the Mexican population in that period of 22 years would be 52.9% while the increase of the population of the United States of America would be 22.0 %.

The rate of increase of the population born in America is even lower if we take into consideration that the United States of America received during that period more immigrants from the rest of the world than Mexico.

Some people in the United States of America say that the Catholic Church and its policies against birth control and abortion have to do with the high rate of population increase of Mexico. This is not true for several reasons:

- First, the percentage of children born out of wedlock is too high and this is not what the Catholic Church recommends.

- Second, after the Mexican Revolution the influence of the Catholic Church in Mexico was reduced significantly.

- Third, there are many Catholic Countries where the increase of the population is not so high. During the same period of 22 years discussed before, in the following predominantly Catholic European countries the increase of the population was much lower than those of Mexico and the United States of America:

  o France (from 54.9 millions to 60.9 millions that means 10.9 %).

o Spain (from 38.4 millions to 40.4 millions that means 5.1%).

o Italy from 56.4 millions to 58.1millions, that means 3.0 %.)

In the country where the Pope lives the increase in population was the lowest of the five countries considered.

Some Mexicans say that the reason for the high increase of the Mexican population was too much music, too much Mariachi, too much eating tacos, too much tequila and too much happiness. That could have been true in part for the past. But now the Mexican Government and many Mexicans have great concern for their population situation. One of their most important activities is to create new jobs. They know that for the economy of the Country it is too bad to raise children that after grown up go to contribute to the economies of other countries.

The Mexicans are disappointed by the fact that many Mexicans have to emigrate because they do not find the jobs they want in their own Country. The rate of growth of the population of Mexico has been reduced dramatically in the last years. In the urban areas of Mexico the rate of birth has been reduced even more rapidly than in the rural areas. It is probable that the supply of emigrants from Mexico to the United States of America will continue for a while, but not for a long time in the future.

On the other hand, one of the reasons for the lower rate of birth in the United States of America is that the high cost of living in this Country requires that husband and wife work full time. The income of one person is not enough to pay the mortgage of a house; the monthly payment, the maintenance and operation of two cars, food, clothing and the rest of the expenses that modern life has. When women know that they have full financial responsibility in the home, it is not easy for them to decide to get pregnant and have children. Even one child is a great complication for many women.

The population of Mexico grew too fast because birth control was limited. In the United States of America the growth of the population was low because birth control was more practiced. This was compensated by immigration, because the strong economy of the United States of America needs to hire immigrants to satisfy its manpower requirements.

The population of Mexico is a young population. The population of the United States of America is an old population. That means that the percentage of population younger than 15 years of age in Mexico is much higher than the percentage of population younger than 15 years of age in the United States of America. Young people accept jobs in the agricultural fields and some industries that old people do not want.

The population of the country that won territory grew slower. The population of the country that lost almost half of its territory grew faster. Because the Mexican economy is not strong many Mexicans prefer to migrate to a country where they can find better jobs with better salaries.

So, these are some of the historical roots of the migration problems between the United States of America and Mexico presented at the beginning of the Third Millennium.

7   From the Discovery of the Americas to the End of the Cold War

This chapter presents a brief review of some of the America and the World more relevant historic events previous to the Third Millennium including: the Discovery of the Americas, the Conquest of the Americas, the Independence of the thirteen English colonies, the America's Corner Stone Documents, the Monroe Doctrine, the French Napoleonic Wars, the American Civil War, the United States of America as a World Power, the First World War, the Second World War, the United Nations, the Cold War, the Korean War, the Cuban Missile Crisis, and the Vietnam War.

The Discovery of the Americas

The first discoverers and conquerors of the Americas were the Spaniards because the Kings of Spain, Ferdinand and Elizabeth, were the sponsors of Christopher Columbus voyages.

In October 12 of 1492, Christopher Columbus arrived to a small island that he called San Salvador because he considered that it saved their lives after several months in an unknown ocean. It is not clear which is this small island where the discovery of the Americas took place.

It could be one of the Lesser Antilles, one of the Bahamas, or one of the Turks Islands.

Columbus continued traveling and later landed at the island that he named La Hispaniola (today Dominican Republic and Haiti.) Columbus left 40 men at a fort he built there in the North of what it is today Haiti and called the fort the "Natividad" or "La Navidad" (Christmas).

On his second trip in 1493, Columbus found that the fort and the people he left in La Hispaniola had vanished. However, new settlements were established in La Hispaniola and other islands that we know today as the Antilles, which include Cuba and Puerto Rico. The Spanish conquerors Hernan Cortes and Juan Ponce de Leon departed later from these islands to explore and conquest what it is today Mexico and Florida.

The Conquest of the Americas

The Spaniards arrived to conquest the Americas after almost eight centuries of war with the "moros" (Muslim invaders from Arab Countries and North Africa) who had occupied parts of Spain since the seventh century. This very long war is called in Spain "La Reconquista" (the re-conquest.)

For the Native Americans, the Spanish warriors in horse back with pistols and "arcabuces" or rifles, were something they had never seen before believing at first that they were superior beings. The Native Americans were convinced at the beginning that they could not win a fight against them. *See Related Story One: The Inca Empire and the Spaniards,* in the Third Part of this Book.

The gold, silver and other products that the Spaniards took from the Americas helped them to become the first world power at the beginning of the Sixteenth Century.

In 1607, when the English were in Jamestown, Virginia establishing their first colony, the Spaniards had more than one hundred years with permanent colonies in the Americas.

It is interesting to note that in 1607 there were Spanish colonies already established in the South, the West and the Gulf of Mexico Regions of what it is today the United States of America. Spanish was the first European language spoken in the territory of what it is today the United States of America.

The first English settlement at Jamestown, Virginia is very important in history. Jamestown is where we can find the origin or the beginning of the thirteen colonies that later became the United States of America. In Jamestown also began the British Empire; the Great British Empire that later included colonies in North America, parts of South and Central America, the West Indies, India and other parts of Asia, Australia, part of Africa, and part of the Middle East.

This clearly explains why the Queen Elizabeth II of England had accepted the two invitations that the American authorities have made to her to visit Jamestown, Virginia: one in May of 1957 to celebrate the 350th anniversary, and the other in May of 2007 to celebrate the 400th anniversary of the foundation of this colony.

The conquest and colonization of Brazil by Portugal is an important chapter in the history of the Americas. However, it has been out of the scope of this book because it considers mainly the interactions between the countries of North America. The immigration of people from Portugal and Brazil to the United States of America is very important.

But the author considered that it is not part of the complex migration situation studied and discussed in this book.

The relations between Spain and England deteriorated rapidly after the English initiated their exploration of North America. Spain did not like the competition of other European countries in the "New Continent."

Philip II, King of Spain, the most powerful ruler in the world in the Sixteenth Century was angry because many settlements in his colonies and many ships, that were transporting gold, silver and other goods from the Americas to Spain, were attacked in the seas by pirate ships that were sponsored by the English. *See Related Story 2: Pirates of the Caribbean,* in the Third Part of this book.

In 1588, Philip II sent a great naval fleet called the "Armada Invencible" or the "Invincible Fleet" to conquer England. The main objective of this operation was to punish England for the pirate attacks to the Spanish colonies and ships. Another objective was to reconvert England to the Catholicism. However, Philip II was not successful; the Armada was defeated in the English Channel by the English fleet, and the rest of the ships were destroyed and sunk by unexpected bad weather conditions. This disaster initiated the weakening of Spain and the strengthening of England as world powers.

France established colonies in North America that were too close to the English colonies. A rivalry between France and England started.

The strengthening of England as a colonial power continued for the next two centuries, but in 1776 it suffered a set back with the independence of thirteen of its American colonies that came to be the United States of America.

The Independence of the Thirteen English Colonies in America

During the age of the great discoveries the European powers claimed for them the lands they found in their explorations around the world. Apparently the Europeans never thought about the rights of the people who were living there before their arrival. The Spaniards said that they wanted to convert the aborigines to the only true religion, the Christian Roman Catholic, to save their souls. They also said that they wanted to civilize them and to give them a better and more important language.

The Europeans justified their colonization effort saying that they needed to expand their territory; they claimed the discovered land in the name of the king of the country that sponsored the exploration and conquest. They also said that they wanted to civilize the aborigines, because they considered that they were uncivilized.

The Imperial colonial powers made a big mistake. They did not give the same rights that they had in their countries to the people in the colonies. There were two laws; the laws for the countries, and the laws for the colonies made by the countries without the participation of the people of the colonies.

In the 1770s England wanted to get more taxes from its American colonies, which were under an absolute control.

The colonists became tired of this because their economies were becoming stronger, and they were paying too high taxes imposed by laws made without their participation. They did not like the abusive laws that the English made for the colonies.

In 1773 England put a new tax on tea that the colonists considered very high. The colonists became very disappointed with this new law. Some colonists were so angry that they broke into a ship that was loading tea in Boston, Massachusetts, and threw all the tea into the water. This act of rebellion became called the "Boston Tea Party."

In 1774, the colonists met in Philadelphia, Pennsylvania and decided no to buy more English goods. They wrote a letter to the King of England expressing their disappointment with the English laws. At this meeting the colonists understood that the situation was difficult, and that a war with England could come. At this meeting Patrick Henry said his famous sentence "give me liberty or give me dead."

In 1775, the English began an effort to recover the control of the colonies. The American Revolution began. In July 1776 representatives of the thirteen English colonies met at what today is Independence Hall in Philadelphia, Pennsylvania. In July 4, 1776 the Declaration of Independence was approved and signed by representatives of the thirteen colonies.

A long war against England was initiated. General George Washington was the leader of the Colonial Army. In 1783 the war ended. The American colonies, with the help of France, won the Independence War.

England and France had colonies in North America, some of these colonies were neighbors and there were frictions between them. England and France became rivals in the conquest of North America. During the American independence war the King of France thought that it would be a good idea to help George Washington and the American revolutionaries.

France sent General La Fayette to fight and help the American Revolution. They won. England lost thirteen American colonies, and became weaker. Apparently this was very good for France.

The king of France did not know that the American Revolution was a real revolution that would change the world. When General La Fayette officers and soldiers went back to France they brought copies of the American Declaration of Independence and they had assimilated the ideas of Thomas Jefferson and the United States of America Founding Fathers. In July 14 of 1789, the people of Paris destroyed La Bastille. Later the absolutist Kingdom of France was over. The King and the Queen of France lost their heads in the Guillotine. A Republic was established. Later the chaos and the terror went to France. After that came the dictatorship of Napoleon Bonaparte and his wars.

The first colonies in the Americas to get independence were the United States of America, probably because they were the first colonies to assimilate the European culture, technology, discoveries and knowledge; and to develop a unique philosophy about freedom. The peoples of these colonies were angry for the continuous taxation without representation from the colonial Metropolis.

It is difficult to know the origin of the strong philosophy for freedom of the founding fathers of the United State of America. Some historians believe that it was born in England. But it is possible that it was born in America, in the interaction between the first English settlers and the Native Americans that helped them and even saved them from starvation with their turkeys; the same turkeys with which we commemorate Thanks Giving Day. It is possible that the ideas that changed the world came from the Natives of North America. It is interesting to observe that this people did not belong to great empires, like the ones of the Incas or the Aztecs, they were very independent people. Most of them never were slaves and died fighting to defend their land.

There is a parallel between Patrick Henry's phrase "Give me liberty or give me death" and the behavior of the Natives of North America.

After the United States of America got independence, the second colony in the Americas to get independence was Haiti. In this country more than ninety per cent of the population was formed of slaves. They worked hard, but no for them; they worked hard for their masters overseas. They were desperate for living in these conditions.

There is a relation between the Independence of Haiti and that of the United States of America. About six hundred Haitians were brought to the United States of America by French General La Fayette to fight in the American Revolution. When they arrived back to Haiti, they had received military training, had knowledge of the Declaration of Independence of the United States of America and of the ideas that gave origin to the American Revolution.

A successful slave revolt was organized a few years after the independence of the United States of America that even Napoleon Bonaparte could not defeat. It is difficult to understand why this French colony, where more than ninety per cent of the inhabitants were slaves, continue that way after the French Revolution and its slogan of "liberty, equality, fraternity." More difficult to understand is that the French forced this poor people to pay with interest, after Haiti independence, for the "investments" they had made there, forgetting that the Haiti's slaves had worked for them without salary for many years.

For the English it was not easy to accept that they had lost the thirteen American English colonies. They fought back in the British American War between 1812 and 1815. In 1812, English troops invaded the United States of America. They reached Washington D.C. and put the White House in flames. The White House had to be evacuated. Today we can see in Washington D.C. the building were the President of the United States of America had his office while the White House was repaired from the damage made by the arsonist English troops.

The last battle of this war was fought in New Orleans in January 18, 1815 where 8,000 British troops fought against 5,000 American troops. The battle was won by the Americans after more than 2,000 British soldiers were killed. It is interesting that a peace agreement, known as the Treaty of Ghent, was signed at the end of 1814; unfortunately, the news of that agreement had not arrived to New Orleans on the day of the "Battle of New Orleans." This problem of communications had a cost of more than 2000 lives to the British troops, who after this battle never came back to the United States of America as enemies.

The America's Corner Stone Documents

Thomas Jefferson was the writer of the Declaration of the Independence of the United States of America that says that:

The colonies were free and independent from England.

All men are created equal.

All men are endowed by their Creator with certain unalienable rights that nobody can take away; these rights are life, liberty, and the pursuit of happiness.

The people tell their government what to do.

The government must do what the people say.

If the people want to, they can form a new government.

Since July 1776 the United States of America organized their internal governments, but there was not a strong national government until the Constitution of the United States of America was promulgated in 1787. It establishes the three branches of the Federal government: Legislative, Executive and Judicial. It also establishes the three levels of Government: Federal, State, and Local.

In 1791 a group of ten amendments to the Constitution, known as the Bill of Rights, were approved, because the people had not forgotten the abuses of the English Government, and wanted to be protected against possible abuses by a strong Federal Government. The first five amendments refer to the general rights of the people. They are: (1) Freedom of religion, freedom of speech and freedom of assemble. (2) Right of the People to keep and bear arms. (3) No soldiers quartered in houses without the owner consent in time of peace. (4) Right of the people to be secured in their persons, homes or personal effects against searches and seizures. (5) No person has to be a witness against himself, or be twice in jeopardy for the same offense, or deprived of his property without just compensation.

The amendments 6, 7, and 8 of the Bill of Rights refer to the rights of the people behind the Justice system: (6) Right of an accused to criminal trial by Jury. (7) Right of trial by jury in suits at common law. (8) Not excessive fines shall be imposed, nor cruel and unusual punishments inflicted.

The last two amendments of the Bill of Rights clarify that there are more rights and more powers than those mentioned in the constitution for the Federal government that are reserved to the States and to the people: (9) There are other rights retain by the people that are not mentioned in this Constitution. (10) The powers not delegated to the United States by the Constitution, nor prohibited by it to the States, are reserved to the States respectively or to the people.

After the Bill of Rights, seventeen additional amendments have been made to the Constitution of the United States of America. These are the America's Corner Stone Documents that have given origin to the most stable government on earth; and have been an inspiration for many other countries.

The Monroe Doctrine

After the Spanish colonies in the western hemisphere won their independence from Spain they were very weak countries. The United States of America recognized the new countries and initiated commercial relations with them, which had been forbidden by Spain before.

It was known that the King of Spain was planning to re-conquest some of the former Spanish colonies and that other European nations were planning to go there. The President of the United States of America understood that any intervention of the Europeans in any country of the western hemisphere would be problem for all the countries of this hemisphere.

In December 2 of 1823, the President of the United of America James Monroe, in his annual message to Congress, presented a policy that later was know as the Monroe doctrine. It established that the United States of America will oppose any further colonization by the Europeans in the western hemisphere, and any interposition in the affairs of these countries with the purpose of oppressing or controlling them.

The Monroe Doctrine was very important for the stability of the Americas, especially for that of the small countries of Latin America that did not have capacity to defend themselves from the big powers. For the Latin American countries America came to be like the big brother that guaranteed their independence. However, the interventions made by the United States of America in some countries of the western hemisphere, and the good and close relations that today exist among the countries of Europe and the countries of the Americas have made this document irrelevant.

The French Napoleonic Wars

In 1799, Napoleon Bonaparte, the famous Commander of French forces in Italy that also got prestige after defeating Austrian forces, seized power in France and established a new Constitution and a regimen called the Consulate. Napoleon as First Consul got dictatorial powers. He almost finished with the chaos posterior to the French Revolution but maintained some of its revolutionary conquests. In 1802 an amendment to the Constitution made Napoleon Consul for life, another constitutional amendment in 1804 made Napoleon the Emperor of France as Napoleon the First.

In December of 1805, Napoleon forces attacked the Austro-Russian army and defeated it in the battle of Austerlitz. In 1806, Napoleon took the kingdom of Naples and named his older brother Joseph Bonaparte as King of Naples. In 1807, Napoleon took the Dutch Republic and transformed it in the Kingdom of Holland with his brother Louis Bonaparte as King. Later he fought the Prussia-Russia Confederation Army and destroyed it. Later Napoleon took the Kingdom of Portugal.

In 1808 Napoleon conquered Spain and put his brother Joseph Bonaparte as King of Spain and put one of his brothers in law as King of Naples; Napoleon had problems in Spain, where there were many rebels.

In 1809 Napoleon conquered what now are Slovenia, Croatia, and Bosnia-Herzegovina. In 1810 Napoleon annexed to the Empire the North of Germany.

Napoleon ruled all the conquered countries under a Napoleonic Code that gave to the people of these countries many of the freedoms and social laws of the French Revolution.

In 1812, Napoleon invaded Russia. The Russians allowed him to enter the country. They burned the possible shelters that Napolonic forces would need and attacked him during the Russian winter. Napoleon lost his armies and lost his prestige after this disaster. All European armies united against him. Napoleon made efforts to recover the power and to fight the rebel countries. But in 1814 his generals refused to continue fighting for him. It looked that Napoleon Bonaparte was finished. He abdicated and was exiled in the island of Elba.

In 1815, Napoleon escaped from the Island of Elba and went to Paris where he found support from military people that had served with him. French politicians did not like him, and the European Countries did not like him. He organized some troops and went to Belgium, where he was defeated in the Battle of Waterloo. He was taken prisoner and exiled to the island of Saint Helena where he died on May 5 of 1821.

It is interesting to observe that the objective of Napoleon Bonaparte was to conquer all Europe and if possible the whole world, but one of the results of his wars was the independence of Spain's colonies in the Americas.

The great Spanish Empire collapsed rapidly after the French Emperor Napoleon Bonaparte invaded Spain. The Spanish people fought the French occupiers and defeated Napoleon at the end. But the Metropolis of the Spanish Empire became very weak and a critic situation was presented after the French occupation. Being occupied, Spain lost its authority over the colonies. At this time, the Spanish American colonies took advantage of this situation, and under the leadership of Simon Bolivar and Jose de San Martin, they won the independence war in South America. Likewise, Mexico and Central America fought for their independence. In a short period of time, Spain lost all its colonies in the Americas, with the exception of Cuba and Puerto Rico.

Napoleon Bonaparte, who commanded the best artillery of his times, said that the country with the best artillery establishes the rules of international moral. Adolfo Hitler, and admirer of Napoleon, who commanded the best military of his time probably also thought that the country with the best military establishes the rules of international moral.

Fortunately, now we have the Organization of the United Nations to establish the rules of international moral. This international organization does not have military forces, and depends on the contributions of its member countries to enforce the international law. This is a very difficult task, but the United Nations is a very useful Organization. It would be too dangerous for the world if the country with the most powerful nuclear arsenal believes that it can establish the rules of international moral.

In 1861, the liberal government of Benito Juarez in Mexico stopped the payment of interest to the European loans. French ruler Napoleon III thought that it was a good idea to occupy

Mexico to control its finances. He offered to the Mexicans to establish a kingdom there and also offered protection from his powerful neighbor the United States of America.

In 1861 the French invaded Mexico. They took the Port of Veracruz and marched to Puebla where they found heavy resistance from President Benito Juarez Mexican forces. The French sent 30,000 additional troops and conquered Puebla. Later they conquered Mexico City and brought Maximilian of Austria with the title of Maximilian the First, as Emperor of Mexico. The French transformed the old Castle of Chapultepec in the Palace of Chapultepec where Maximilian was installed with the luxury of an European king.

The United States of America did not like the French intervention, which was against the Monroe Doctrine, and supported President Juarez Regimen that continue ruling part of Mexico, but the United States of America did not help Juarez because they were in big trouble with their own Civil War.

In 1867 the French withdrew most of their troops from Mexico because they needed them in Europe to solve urgent military problems there. Juarez's forces took advantage of the situation and re-conquered the country gradually. General Porfirio Diaz liberated Mexico City. The Emperor of Mexico Maximilian of Austria the First was taken prisoner in Queretaro and executed by a firearms squadron in 1867.

Maximilian of Austria loved the Mexican music. He organized groups of Mexican musicians to play their music in the weddings of important people. The French called these musicians "marriages" because they played in the weddings. The Mexican called them "mariachis."

The American Civil War

The American Civil War was fought between 1861 and 1865. It was a war between the Northern States or the Union, and the Southern states called the Confederacy. It was a terrible war where more than half million soldiers died.

The causes of the American Civil war were disagreements, mainly about slavery and taxes, between the North and the South of the United States of America. The North was industrialized and wanted taxes to protect its industrial products from overseas competition. Their industrial activity was favored by the arrival of immigrants from Europe. They did not want slave labor.

On the other hand, the South economy was based in the export of cotton; their production of cotton was based in slave labor. They imported industrial products and were angry by the high import taxes that were established. The Southerners did not want to buy industrial goods made by the Northerners because they preferred imported goods.

The states of the North created more dependency from the Federal government and felt that they were part of the Union. The States of the South were more independent, and started looking at the Federal government in the same way that the colonists saw England before the independence of the United States of America.

Slavery was an abominable institution and a shame for mankind. African people were forced to come to America to work for landlords that were their masters. They did not have any rights or any freedom. Slave owners bought and sold the slaves as if they were their property. Slavery was an old institution that comes from the early days of history, but it did not fit with America; it did not fit with the Declaration of Independence. It did not fit with the philosophy of the Founding Fathers of the United States of America.

When we study carefully the Declaration of Independence and the Constitution of the United States of America, we arrive to the conclusion that these two documents are very important not only for the American people, but for all mankind. The founding fathers of this country were the best poets and philosophers of freedom and liberty.

It is difficult to understand that slavery continued and was legal for more than eight decades in a country ruled and inspired by these documents. But if we read the Bible's gospels and take into consideration the importance that Christianity has had in Europe and in the Americas, it is even more difficult to understand why we have had two millenniums of Christianity but less than two centuries without slavery.

It is possible that slavery could have been abolished only after the invention of the steam engine and the other engines that followed it during the industrial revolution. Theologians, philosophers and even politicians always knew and understood that slavery was wrong and immoral; but for economic reasons it was tolerated. What a shame for us and for our ancestors.

The engineers with their engines and not the theologians, philosophers or the sociologists made possible the end of slavery. This could be the reason for which the industrialized North of the United States of America supported the abolition of slavery and the South that was not so industrialized fought against it.

In 1861, Abraham Lincoln became President. He and the Northern states were against slavery and they wanted to end the system of slavery. They established taxes that helped their factories to grow.

The Southern states said that they needed slaves to work in their agricultural lands. They were against the taxes because they made their products more expensive and difficult to sell overseas. They left the Union and formed a Confederacy. The Civil War began in 1861.

In 1863, more than 51,000 Union and Confederate soldiers died in Gettysburg, Pennsylvania. Four months after that battle Lincoln spoke in the dedication of the Gettysburg National Cemetery. Lincoln finished his dedication speech saying "...this dead shall no have died in vain; that this nation, under God, shall have a new birth of freedom, and that this government of the people, by the people, for the people shall no perish from the earth."

President Lincoln did not want that the Country be divided; he wanted to save the Union. He fought the Confederacy during four years. Lincoln did not want a country half free and half slave. In 1863 President Lincoln signed the Emancipation Proclamation. But not all the slaves became free. An amendment to the Constitution was required because slaves were property. And the Constitution protected property. At least this was what some lawyers of those days said.

On February 1, 1865 Congress passed the XIII Amendment that was ratified on December 18, 1866: "Neither slavery nor involuntary servitude, except as punishment for crime whereof the party shall have been duly convicted, shall exist in the United States, or any place subject to their jurisdiction."

The City of Richmond, Virginia, that was the Capital of the Confederation, was attacked by the Union forces and abandoned by its defenders on April 2, 1865. Lincoln knew that the war was won and that the Union was saved.

On April 14, 1865 President Abraham Lincoln was assassinated in Washington D.C. in the Ford Theater by a famous actor that was angry because President Lincoln won the civil war. During the American Civil war President Abraham Lincoln with his emancipation policy was the right man with the right policy at the right time. He was assassinated because some of the slave's masters that had invested an important part of their capital in slaves did not like him.

The United States of America as a World Power

The United States of America declared the war to Spain after the American war ship *Maine* exploited and sunk in the harbor of Havana, Cuba on February 15, 1898. At that time the Cuban rebels were fighting for their independence, and had established control over a great part of the Cuban territory. The result of this war was that Spain lost Cuba and Puerto Rico, its last colonies in the Americas, and the Philippines. Today, we know that the explosion of the war ship *Maine* was an accident and not an attack by Spain.

Since the Cuban revolutionaries were winning the war to obtain Cuba's independence they got it very soon. Puerto

Rico and The Philippines became United States territories. The Philippines got their independence in the twentieth century, after the Second World War. Puerto Rico is a Free Associate Commonwealth of the United States of America. *See Related Story 6: The Commonwealth of Puerto Rico,* in the Third Part of this book.

In one century Spain changed from a world power to a weak country defeated by a former English colony, the United States of America, a country that after a devastated civil war, with more than half million soldiers killed, reorganized its military forces and started its roll as an important country in the world.

In the twentieth century the United States of America became a strong member of the International Community. It was an important partner in the defeat of Germany in the First World War (1914-1918).

The First World War

In August 1914, a World War began after the assassination of the Duke Francis Ferdinand of the Austro Hungary Empire. At the beginning the war was between the Allied Power countries integrated by England, France and Russia against the Central Powers Germany and Austria-Hungary.

Later Belgium, Serbia, Montenegro, Italy and Japan joined to the Allied Powers. The Ottoman Empire joined the Central Powers in 1914, and Bulgaria joined them in 1915.

This war was called the Great War or the World War because many of the European countries participated in it, as well as some countries of the rest of the world and because more than 10 million people were killed. Only after the 1939 conflict was called the Second World War the conflict of 1914-1918 was called the First World War.

For three years the First World War was without much progress from each side. Many trenches protected with barbed wire in both sides maintained the troops immobilized.

In 1917, the United States of America entered in the war and helped the Allied Powers of England, France, Russia and other countries to win. The war ended in November of 1918. The United States of America became a more important world power after its participation in this war.

This war changed the map of Europe. The Ottoman and Austro-Hungary Empires collapsed with this defeat. Despite that Russia was in the winner side, the Bolshevik Revolution of 1917 finished with the Czars Empire and initiated the communist Soviet Union age.

The high costs of this war weakened the European countries. The sanctions imposed by the winners to the defeated countries, mainly to Germany, created the situation that later became the origin of the Second World War.

The First World War was a disaster for the Ottoman Empire, an empire that was several centuries old. The Crusades and the First World War are historical events for which some Muslim countries do not like the Western Powers including the British Empire and the United States of America that they see now as permanent allies.

The Second World War

In 1939, a war started in Europe. This war became the more devastating conflict ever seen by mankind. The war was initiated as a reaction of England and France against Germany's preemptive wars against its neighbors. In 1938, Adolfo Hitler's Nazi Germany annexed Austria and a part of Czechoslovakia. In 1939, Nazi Germany annexed the rest of Czechoslovakia and Poland, with which France had a mutual defense pact. In the first stage of this war the military superiority of Hitler's Nazi Germany was obvious. He almost won the war very quickly. Nazi Germany, with its allies Axis Powers Italy and Japan looked invincible. They had also an alliance with the Soviet Union. But Hitler made a big mistake. He decided to abandon his alliance with the Soviet Union and invaded that country.

During the Second World War, Japan attacked Pearl Harbor, Hawaii in 1941. President Franklin D. Roosevelt called this attack without previous declaration of war "an act of infamy" and decided to join the Allied powers and became their partner in the war effort.

Now the Allied countries had incorporated two giants to their group: The United States of America and the Soviet Union. The United States of America transformed its powerful industrial capacity into the biggest military industry ever known which President Franklin D. Roosevelt called "the Arsenal of Democracy".

The Nazi Germany occupation of Russia was not successful in a short time as Hitler thought. The heroic Russian counter attack, together with the Russian winter, almost finishes with all the German Nazi invaders. Hitler's troops suffered the same fate that Napoleon Bonaparte's troops had suffered more than one hundred years before.

Now the Allied forces were ready to attack Germany. American weapons were sent to the Soviet Union and the European allies. The leadership of British Prime Minister Winston Churchill was very important in all these war efforts; his letters to President Franklin D. Roosevelt convincing him of the importance of the participation of the United States of America in the European theater of this war are important documents and an important part of the history of the Second World War.

The Americans invaded Italy. The Italian people made a revolt against Hitler's ally Benito Mussolini, Il Duce, who was hung in the Milano Square. Finally Germany was invaded by Russia, and France, which had been occupied by Germany, was liberated by American, British and French (resistance) troops. Italy no longer was a German allied. A few weeks later, Germany was defeated. Hitler killed himself in his bunker in Berlin on April 30, 1945. Before his suicide, he married his mistress Eva Brown.

The brutal Hitler's Nazi regimen established many policies against humanity, including a racist policy that killed many innocent people just for their race or origin. Many Jewish and Gipsy people, and people from other nationalities were killed in a massive way by the abominable Nazi regimen.

The objective of Adolfo Hitler in the Second World War was to conquest all Europe and if possible the whole world too. But the result of his wars was the independence of the rest of the British colonies and other European colonies worldwide because, like Napoleon, he made also the colonial metropolis weaker countries.

The war between the United States of America and Japan was a difficult, bloody and long one. Japan surrendered to the United States of America after it was attacked with one atomic bomb in Hiroshima, and another one in Nagasaki. The nuclear age had started. The nuclear attack against Japan happened when only one country had that weapon. Now that the "Nuclear Club" has at least ten partners, a nuclear war could be the end of mankind.

The United States of America occupied Japan after it surrendered. General Douglas Mac Arthur was the Commander of the U.S. occupation forces in Japan. Emperor Hirohito continued as the Emperor of the occupied Japan. To allow Emperor Hirohito to continue was a very good decision because Hirohito had the capacity and the power to help to govern occupied Japan in a peaceful way. The Japan reconstruction and economic recovery was so rapid that it was called a "Miracle". Quite a difference with what happened during the American and coalition forces occupation of Iraq during the years 2003 to 2007. Of course, the situations were very different.

The European powers were successful establishing their overseas empires because part of the rest of the world was impressed by their high level of development and culture, and their military superiority. However, after assimilating in part the European culture, and observing their behavior in the Napoleonic wars and the two World wars, the people from the colonies understood and realized that the Europeans were not the highly civilized people and the smarter people they had thought. They saw that the Europeans were using their civilization and their power to kill and destroy themselves.

The United Nations

After the Second World War, the nations of the world met in San Francisco, California on April 25, 1945 to discuss how to have a world forum to discuss international cooperation and international tensions in order to avoid another disaster like the two World Wars. On October 24, 1945, the chart of the United Nations was approved. The headquarters of the United Nations were established in the city of New York. New Yorkers are proud of that and say that New York City is the capital of the world.

The United Nations has a General Secretary, a Security Council and a General Assembly.

It has several specialized agencies that advice the member countries at their request.

The General Assembly is the maximum authority and is constituted by delegates from all the member countries.

The Security Council is very important because it meets more frequently and is more flexible and operative than the General Assembly. It has 15 members, of which 5 are permanent members with veto power. China, the United States of America, Russia, the United Kingdom and France are the permanent members. It is a problem that India, a country with more than one billion of inhabitants is not a permanent member of the Security Council. Another problem is that Latin America, Africa and Oceania are not permanent members in the Security Council. The inclusion of India, Brazil or Mexico, Nigeria and Australia as permanent members of the Security Council could solve this situation. The number of members of the Security Council could be increase to nineteen. And the number of permanent members could be increased to nine. These have to be fixed to strength the democratic nature of this great and important organization.

The Cold War

After the Second World War, the United States of America and the Soviet Union became the two nuclear world superpowers. These countries after being closely allied in the First and Second World Wars became political enemies. The war between them was called the Cold War. They fought wars in Korea, Vietnam, and Central America. During these wars fought in third countries territories, the developed rich superpowers contributed with the weapons and financing of the hostilities. In the case of Korea and Vietnam, the United States of America also contributed with many troops. Since Korea, Vietnam, and the Central American countries were not rich countries, their contributions to the wars were mainly with troops, and they suffered a great amount of casualties not only military but civil. See *Related Story 7: The Cold War in Central America,* in the Third Part of this book.

We have to arrive to the conclusion that the underdeveloped countries had unwise and complicated politics that allowed the Superpowers to fight their wars in their territories. We can also think that the Superpowers were "smart enough" to fight their wars in the territories of other countries and no in their own territories. A symbol of the Cold War was the

Berlin Wall, which was built by the Soviets to stop the flow of the Germans from communist East Germany to democratic West Berlin. Before the collapse of the Soviet Union, on June 12, 1987, President Ronald Reagan said in Berlin his now famous sentence to the Soviet General Secretary: **"Mr. Gorvachev, tear down this wall."**

The Korean War

Because Japan had occupied the peninsula of Korea after the end of the Second World War, the Soviet Union sent troops to the North of that Country to finish with the Japanese occupation; and the United States of America sent troops to the South to liberate the South of Korea. North Korea became a communist country under the influence of the Soviet Union; and South Korea became a country under the influence of the United States of America. A border between North Korea and South Korea was established in the now famous parallel 38 north.

The Korean War started in 1950 after communist North Korea trespassed the parallel 38, which was the border between both countries and invaded South Korea. North Korea was successful defeating the South Korea resistance, after which President Harry S. Truman decided to go to war to stop the invasion. Second World War hero General Douglas Mac Arthur was the Commander of the American troops.

The North Korean forces continue defeating the South Korean resistance. When the American troops arrived the situation was very difficult. The problem became more complicated when communist China decided to go to North Korea and participated in the war. At one point the North Korean troops controlled almost the whole Korean peninsula.

The use of nuclear weapons against North Korea and China was discussed. Soviet Union's Joseph Stalin became nervous, and sent Soviet bombers to the East of the Soviet Union, closer to America.

President Truman and General Mac Arthur did not agree about how to continue the course of the war, and President Truman asked General Mac Arthur for his resignation on April 11, 1951.

The war continued for more than two years with strong fighting and heavy casualties from both sides and the South Korea territory was recovered from the North Koreans.

Sponsored by the United Nations an armistice agreement was signed in July 1953. A 2.5 miles demilitarized zone was established in parallel 38 North. The United Nations, China and North Korea signed the armistice, but South Korea did not sign it. So theoretically this war has not ended.

The Cuban Missile Crisis

Another important chapter of the Cold War was the Cuban Missile crisis. Fidel Castro initiated his political life as a freedom fighter. He wanted to put out of power Cuban dictator Fulgencio Batista. In 1959 Castro won a revolution. He visited the United States of America, but President Eisenhower did not see him. Vice-President Nixon talked to him, but we do not know what they talked.

A few months later Fidel Castro declared that he was a Marxist and a Leninist and that he has been a communist since his early college days; therefore the Cuban revolution was a Marxist and Leninist movement. Now the Soviet Union had an allied in the Caribbean, in the backyard of the United States of America.

The cooperation between the Soviet Union and Cuba became very strong. President Eisenhower tried to do something to stop it, but the Soviets told him that if he attacked Cuba, they would attack Berlin.

In 1962, President John F. Kennedy was informed that the Soviets were building a missile base in Cuba, and that a Soviet fleet was traveling from the Soviet Union to Cuba with nuclear weapons. President Kennedy saw that the world was in big trouble. The possibility of a nuclear war had never been so close.

It was a very difficult situation. President Kennedy had many discussions with the American military Chief of Staff and top military officials; and with many advisors. An American Invasion of Cuba was one of the possibilities discussed.

President Kennedy decided to tell the Soviets that to avoid a nuclear war the Soviet Fleet had to abandon its mission and go back to the Soviet Union. The Soviet fleet did that, and Fidel Castro became very disappointed.

The Vietnam War

The Vietnam War had a parallel with the Korean War. Communist North Vietnam invaded democratic South

Vietnam and the United States of America decided to support the invaded country. China wanted to demonstrate to the United States of America that this is an area of China influence, not an area of American influence.

Vietnam had fought for its independence against the French that had colonized them at the end of the Nineteenth Century. The economic situation deteriorated under French rule, mainly during World War II. Movements against the French occupation spread and the Vietnam Communist Party coordinated and stimulated these efforts.

The leader Ho Chi Minh finally organized the League for Independence of Vietnam. At the end of the World War II the leader Ho Chi Minh declared the Independence of Vietnam and established the capital of his Government in Hanoi. The French reacted against Ho Chi Minh and retained the control over the South of the Country and formed another Government under Bao Dai of the Nguyen dynasty.

In 1950 Ho Chi Minh Government of North Vietnam was receiving support from the Communist Government of China, and the South Vietnam Government of Bao Dai received support from the French and from the United States of America that was afraid of the growing influence of China in Southeast Asia.

In May 1954, after the French position in Dien Vien Phu was attacked, the French government accepted to discuss a peace agreement. In July 1954 the French agreed, against the United States of America advice, in the withdrawal of the French troops and in the temporary division of Vietnam in North Vietnam and South Vietnam.

The French left, but the United States of America that had been supporting the French continued the struggle. Ngo Dinh Dien, who became the President of the Republic of Vietnam, substituted Bao Dai. He was a strong anti communist and the United States of America continued supporting his war efforts.

In 1959 North Vietnam initiated a war against South Vietnam. There were some communists in South Vietnam that would support the North. The United States of America continue giving support to the Dinh Dien Government in the training of his forces and with military equipment.

In 1965 the United States of America saw that South Vietnam was going to lose the war and sent troops to South Vietnam and started bombing North Vietnam. Ho Chi Minh considered that he could defeat the Americans in the same way that he had defeated the French.

In 1968 Ho Chi Minh launched a simultaneous attack in almost all South Vietnam cities that produced heavy casualties in American and South Vietnam troops, and weakened the Government of the new South Vietnam President Nguyen Van Thieu.

The American People were tired and disappointed with the war. President Lyndon Johnson announced that he will not run for reelection as President, and that he will look for a negotiated end to the Vietnam War.

In 1972 North Vietnam accepted to discuss an end to the war after a second offensive failed. In 1973 an agreement was signed in Paris. The agreement did not stop the North

Vietnam continuation of some attacks. But the last American troops left Vietnam that year.

In 1975 North Vietnam launched an offensive when the United States Troops no longer were there to stop them, and did not have the will to go back. The South Vietnam regimen collapsed and the communists took Saigon. Vietnam was reunited under a communist regimen.

The War of Vietnam could be considered as the first war lost by the United States of America, but the reality is that the United States of America abandoned Vietnam because the Americans did not support that war at the end.

8 The Americas before the Arrival of the Europeans

The Land

The Americas constitute one of the most beautiful parts of the globe. When the people of the rest of the world ignored the existence of the Americas, they missed a beautiful and important part of the planet that only the Native Americans were enjoying, like:

> The great mountains: Andes, Rocky, Appalachian, etc.

> The great rivers and their valleys: Amazon, Mississippi, Colorado, Magdalena, Orinoco, Parana, etc.

> The great lakes: Erie, Ontario, Huron, Michigan and Superior; Titicaca, Maracaibo and Nicaragua.

> The great falls: Niagara, Iguassu and Tequendama.

> The great plains and valleys: of North and South America.

For many centuries the people of Asia, Europe and Africa thought that their continents were the only ones in the world. Because they did not travel far in the seas, they did not know of the existence of other continents at the other side of the oceans. They ignored the existence of North America, South America, Oceania and the Antarctic.

Christopher Columbus not only discovered The Americas in 1492. He opened the oceans, and people could go farther. Soon Ferdinand Magellan and Sebastian Elcano first trip around the World confirmed without doubt that the Earth is a globe. The great discoveries were made and the ignored continents were found. Now we know that planet Earth has a surface of 196.8 millions of square miles, that the oceans have a surface of 138.9 millions of square miles (70.6 %), and that the continental surface has 57.9 millions of square miles (29.4%).

Before the great discoveries, the surface of the known continents was 32.8 millions of square miles, as follows:

Continent	Area in millions of square miles	% of the Earth's continental surface
Asia	17.3	29.88
Africa	11.7	20.20
Europe	3.8	6.56
Total	32.8	56.64

After the great discoveries the following continents were found:

Continent	Area in millions of square miles	% of the Earth's continental surface
North America	9.5	16.41
South America	6.9	11.92
Oceania	3.3	5.70
Antarctica	5.4	9.33
Total	25.1	43.36

The Americas represent 28.33 % (16.41+11.92) of the Earth's continental surface.

The Americas have more than four times the area of Europe. Christopher Columbus discovered something very important and unexpected.

The People

When the western hemisphere was discovered by Christopher Columbus, the Native Americans who had been living in the territories of North and South America for several millenniums were between fifty million and one hundred million of inhabitants. It is not possible to give a more exact figure because after the contact with the Europeans the Native American population was reduced significantly by the diseases brought to the Americas by the Europeans (the Native Americans had not immunity to them), the fights with the conquerors, the chaos created by the occupation of their countries, the assassination of the Native American leaders, and the changes in life style of many Native Americans that had to work very hard for the conquerors in mines or agricultural fields.

The population was incremented later with the children of the Native Americans, the Mestizos and with immigrants from Europe, Asia and Africa; the last ones slaved by the Europeans.

At the beginning of the Third Millennium the population of the Whole Americas is over eight hundred millions of inhabitants. In each one of the two more populated countries of the Earth, China and India, live more people than in the whole Western Hemisphere, as the Americas are also called.

Before the arrival of the Europeans, the Native Americans apparently had no important contacts with the people of other continents. It is believed that before Columbus arrival some of the Native American communities had received visits from people of the North of Europe or Asia, but without the development of permanent interactions or relations with them.

In Peru people tell stories about trips made by Inca explorers to overseas countries. *See Related Story 1: The Inca Empire and the Spaniards,* in the Third Part of this book.

The importance of Colon's arrival to the Americas is that it was the first time that a powerful European Kingdom had contact with these large continents that were isolated for thousands of years from the rest of the world by two big oceans, the Atlantic and the Pacific.

Many ethnic groups of Native Americans lived in small communities and developed their culture and traditions in an isolated way. But there were also great empires and civilizations, like the ones established by the Incas in South America, and the Aztecs and Mayas in what it is now Mexico and Central America.

The Native Americans made utensils and art objects using a variety of materials including gold, silver, ceramic, stone, textiles and others. Many of these objects can be seen today in museums in South, Central and North America. Some of the buildings and water works constructed by them indicate that they had knowledge in architecture and engineering.

They had instruments to follow contour lines in the land, and to construct canals following a given slope. They had also knowledge in agriculture. They had practices to avoid soil erosion when they cultivated in high slope lands, where they constructed terraces following the contour lines. Among their crops were corn, potatoes, tomatoes, sweet potatoes and others that were not known to the Europeans before the discovery of the Americas. They got proteins from turkey, other animals and fish, because they were also very good fishermen.

They had knowledge of medicine, and other related fields, like pharmacy. They crushed leaves and fermented them in dark caves where fungi developed. They applied this paste to heal wounds. It is possible that these fungi were *penicillium* and that they were using penicillin or something similar.

Some of the Native Americans had accountants that used groups of fine cords and knots to record the numbers. They had calendars, among them the famous Aztec Calendar sculpted in stone.

Like the Egyptians, they built many pyramids and temples that are linked to their religious traditions and cult.

At the arrival of the Europeans to America, the Native Americans had primitive transportation systems. They constructed small boats. They did not have horses, but they used the llamas and constructed roads that were paved with stones. Some of these roads are in use today. In South America people call them "el camino del Inca" or "the road of the Inca".

They had some military organizations, but they did not know the firearms. Some of them had wars between themselves but their weapons were primitive (arrows, stones, sticks, hammers, etc.). Their military inferiority facilitated their conquest by the Europeans.

It is not clear what the origin of the Native American people is. It is possible and probable that not all the Native Americans have the same origin.

Most scholars believe that they were descendants of Asian people who came to Alaska through the Bering Strait, and continued traveling in Southward direction to the rest of The Americas.

THIRD PART: RELATED STORIES

1 The Inca Empire and the Spaniards

The Incas

Tupac Yupanqui, son of Pachacutec and father of Huayna Capac is one of the great figures in the history of the Inca Rulers and in the universal history. Tupac Yupanqui was born in the city of Cusco and he was secretly isolated during sixteen years by his father, the Inca Emperor, in the Temple of the Sun or Koricancha, where only his teachers and servants could see him.

Being too young Tupac Yupanqui was married to his sister Mama Oca, a small woman, beautiful and intelligent. After his marriage, his father gave him the order to go to fight rebel enemies of the empire and to conquer new kingdoms. Tupac Yupanqui made a long trip north of Cusco, traveling through different towns and villages that he conquered for the empire including Jauja, Huaylas, Huanuco and Cajamarca. In this last one, he established his headquarters. Later he went down to the coast with the objective of defeating the ruler Chimu Capac and to integrate to the empire the territories that were under his control. He also attacked the city of Chan Chan and disconnected the water supply. After that the thirsty population surrendered. After these victories, Tupac Yupanqui returned to Cusco during the Inti Raymi celebrations where his father received and congratulated him. He spent only two years in Cusco and departed again to accomplish great military missions.

Tupac Yupanqui traveled to the North of the Andes Mountains and conquered the city of Quito where he built a great fortress.   Later he went down to the coast and conquered the Huancavilcas who lived in the Gulf of Guayaquil.   In this war, an incredible naval battle occurred between the Cusco warriors and the Guayaquil warriors who fought in small boats in the beaches surrounded by tropical vegetation.

The conquest of Guayaquil interested Tupac Yupanqui in the naval activity to which he dedicated a great part of his time. He put special attention in the construction of "totora" boats. Totora is a plant abundant in South America that is used by the Native Americans to construct small boats.   Stories say that he made a great fleet with these boats and thousands of men who he selected carefully and departed to explore the Pacific Ocean.   He spent more than a year in this expedition. Many people, including his Father Pachacutec, thought that he had died.

However, Tupac Yupanqui appeared suddenly when nobody was waiting for him.   He made brilliant tales about his adventures in faraway lands.   He brought with him people different from those known in the empire, gold, chairs of metal, leather and horse bones.   He learned about the existence of other empires, other kingdoms and other cultures.

We do not know exactly where Tupac Yupanqui went.   There are speculations that he went to what we know today as the Galapagos Islands, the Hawaiian Islands, the Polynesia, the Fiji islands, and the Salomon islands, Indonesia, and even the Philippines and China.   The Peruvian fishermen tell stories about trips made in recent times from Peru to the Polynesia in small boats.

After six years of wars, explorations and conquests, Tupac Yupanqui returned to Cusco.   He traveled through the

Gran Chimu lands and spent several days praying in the Pachacamac Temple. In Cusco, Tupac Yupanqui introduced his son Huayna Capac to his father the Emperor Pachacutec, who was very happy to meet his grandson who he loved very much thereafter.

The old Pachacutec had a great capacity to rule the Inca Empire, and with the strong support that he received from his son Tupac Yupanqui, the empire reached a level of prosperity and development never seen before. Thanks to the conquests of Tupac Yupanqui, the Inca Empire or Tahuantinsuyo was very strong and powerful in what we know as the year 1480 A.D. In this year, his son Huayna Capac became the Emperor of the Incas.

Huayna Capac did not have time for new explorations or conquests during his first years as Emperor, and he spent all his time consolidating the giant empire he had inherited. However, he made some conquests later, mainly in the South, in territories that today belong to Chile and Argentina.

Despite that the capital of the empire was in Cusco, where his son Huascar lived, Huayna Capac spent too much time in the city of Quito that became almost another capital, where he had another marriage and had another son named Atahualpa. In Cusco, Huascar was considered the legitimate son and the heir of the empire. In Quito, Atahualpa was considered the heir of the Inca Empire. Atahualpa and Huascar became enemies and had wars between them because both wanted to be the Inca Emperor. In this fight, Huascar was killed and Atahualpa became the survivor.

The Conquest by the Spaniards

The Spanish conqueror Francisco Pizarro became a wealthy man in Panama. He learned a lot about a great empire from natives who had traveled to the Pacific South coast and talked to him about it. He wanted to organize an expedition to go to conquest this empire, but the Governor of Panama did not authorize him because it was too dangerous.

In 1528, Francisco Pizarro made a trip to Spain and got a Royal authorization and the nomination of Governor of the lands known to the Spaniards as Peru where this great empire, known to the natives as the Inca Empire, existed.

In May of 1532, Francisco Pizarro arrived to Peru to initiate its conquest. He got information from the natives indicating that Atahualpa was near the city of Cajamarca and that Huascar had been killed recently in the war between the two brothers. The trip to Cajamarca was very difficult. It took them two months to travel the 200 miles between Piura, where they arrived by ship, and Cajamarca. They traveled through rope suspended bridges made by the Incas, which were designed to pass with llamas, no with horses and canyons.

Atahualpa knew that Pizarro and his men were there. Pizarro received visits of natives sent by Atahualpa with some gifts. Pizarro thought that the visits were from Atahualpa intelligence people who wanted to know who they were, how many, and what were their intentions. During this trip, Pizarro also became friend of some natives who were enemies of Atahualpa.

When Pizarro arrived at Cajamarca, he found out that Atahualpa was not there. Pizarro sent a message to Atahualpa indicating that he wanted to talk with him in the name of the King of Spain. Atahualpa answered that the next day he will go to see him and that they can be his guests at a lodge close to Cajamarca square.

Atahualpa arrived the next day, but he decided to spend the night in a place about one mile from Cajamarca. He sent a message to the Spaniards telling them that he was tired and that he would see them the next day. The Spaniards answered that they had prepared supper for him and that they would like to see him that night. Finally, Atahualpa arrived seated in a portable throne carried by the empire principals and "caciques" and preceded by three hundred men who were cleaning the way Atahualpa was going to follow; he was also followed by about five thousand men who did not have weapons.

A Catholic priest initiated the conversation with Atahualpa. The priest told Atahualpa that they were sent there by the King of Spain in order to instruct him about their religion. Soon after, the priest asked Atahualpa if he wanted to become a Christian and gave him a bible telling him that it was the word of God. Atahualpa put the book close to his ears and threw it to the floor furiously, telling them that he could not hear anything.

Atahualpa told them that he knew who they were and demanded that they gave back all the goods that they had taken from his people, pay for the damage done and abandon his land. Atahualpa talked to his principals and advisors and there were many conversations among them. Suddenly, the priest told the Spaniards that it was better not to wait anymore. Pizarro commanded his soldiers to start shutting, what they did immediately. Since the natives had no weapons, they were easily defeated. The principals who were with the Emperor never abandoned him, choosing to be killed protecting him. Then the Spaniards took Atahualpa as a prisoner.

The next day, the Spaniards found the soldiers who traveled with Atahualpa and defeated them easily. They found Atahualpa palace and found lots of gold and silver objects and took many of them. When Atahualpa saw the Spaniards taking the gold and the silver objects, he offered them more in exchange for his liberty and abandoning his land. A rescue was agreed, and Atahualpa made a line in a wall indicating the level to which the room would be filled with gold and silver objects. It took various months until the agreed rescue was accumulated. During this period, Atahualpa was treated with the considerations the Spaniards thought he deserved. The priest told Atahualpa that his land belonged to the Kingdom of Spain because the Pope had given the territories in the Pacific coast of South America to Spain, and the territories in the Atlantic coast of South America to Portugal. Atahualpa asked: who is that mad man who gave away territories that do not belong to him?

Finally the agreed rescue was accumulated. The Spaniards had to put Atahualpa in liberty. He had accepted to be a Christian and to be subdued by the Kingdom of Spain. Pizarro and the Spaniards wanted to free Atahualpa, but the priest told them that he had to be executed because he threw the Bible to the floor and also said that the Pope was a mad man. Atahualpa was executed in August of 1533. The Atahualpa rescue room can be visited today in the city of Cajamarca, Peru.

Twenty per cent of the stolen gold and silver was sent to the Spanish Crown to pay for the one-fifth royal tax. With that measure, the conquerors considered honest assets the gold and silver that they had taken from the Incas. It is believed that part of the gold and silver, stolen from the Incas, was stolen again by the pirates, when it was being sent to Spain. *See Related Story 2: Pirates of the Caribbean.*

2 Pirates of the Caribbean

The Spanish ships transporting gold, silver, and other treasures from the Spanish American colonies to Europe were frequently attacked during the XVII and XVIII centuries. The attackers were pirates. The Caribbean Sea was the area preferred by these pirates because they had bases in Jamaica. Most of these pirates were English, but there were also French, Dutch and Portuguese. These pirates were real felons without law or God. They were supported by the enemies of Spain, among them the English Kingdom, which awarded some of them like the infamous Sir Francis Drake.

The activities of these pirates were diverse. They arrived to the Spanish colonies to steal, to loot, to smuggle, and to have fun. One of their objectives was to break the trade monopoly that Spain had with its colonies. They made trade with food, cocoa and other agricultural products that they changed for English manufactures. They went there also looking for women.

In some cases the population was no loyal to Spain and made business with these pirates. They traded with them and received them as great customers in cantinas, bars and bordellos. Other times, they were received as enemies. There were serious battles where many of the folks and the pirates died. When the pirates defeated the folks killing the men that fought them they stole whatever they could, raped women, looted churches and departed to the seas in their ships. Nine months later the masculine population started to be replaced, in some cases with blue eyes children.

In April 1666, the Governor of Costa Rica Don Juan Lopez de la Flor, received a message from the Royal Audience of

Panama informing him that an expedition had departed from the English Colony of Jamaica commanded by the "admirals" Mansfield and Morgan. Their objective was to attack Central America and to establish a passage between the Atlantic and the Pacific oceans.

The pirates arrived first to Panama and then to Limon, a port in the Atlantic coast of Costa Rica that the Native Americans called Cariari. They interned into the country and took a village with the name of Matina. They took some prisoners that they forced to serve them as guides. A Native American, with the name Esteban Yapiri escaped and sent a message to the Governor in the city of Cartago informing him that more than six hundred pirates were going there to conquest that city that was the Capital of the Province of Costa Rica during the colony.

The Governor ordered the defense and prepared an army of three hundred soldiers recruited in the valleys of Barva, Aserri and Curridabat. This army was commanded by Major Don Alonso de Bonilla and went to Matina with their arcabuces or rifles.

Mansfield and Morgan arrived to the town of Turrialba where they learned that the Governor was preparing an army to fight them. In Turrialba, the pirates occupied the church, the city hall and several homes and farms. They killed cattle to feed themselves. They were initiating a big party when they heard the shuts that the soldiers of Don Alonso de Bonilla were continuously firing to them. The pirates were scared by the attack and ran away; they went back to Matina. Later, when they knew that the Governor sent more troops to follow them, they ran away to the sea.

In June 1676, when the Governor of Costa Rica was Don Juan Francisco Saenz, eight hundred pirates arrived again to Matina. The Governor Saenz went to fight them with five hundred men of Spanish background armed with arcabuces or rifles and two hundred Native American men armed with arcs and arrows. After a bloody battle the Governor army defeated them. The pirates ran away. They left more than two hundred pirates killed and many injured.

These visits by the pirates made difficult the development of the Atlantic coast of Costa Rica. The people moved from this coast and went to places that were far enough from the areas attacked by the pirates. They established settlements in the higher lands that have a better climate. They also moved to the Pacific coast of Costa Rica, where the climate is more favorable than in the Atlantic coast, and where they thought the pirates would not arrive. But they did.

After the pirates learned that the Spaniards had colonized the Pacific coast of South America and found lots of gold and silver, they went there. They attacked the Peruvian port of Callao and the city of Lima in various opportunities and looted the houses of the rich people and the churches. Because it was very difficult for them to bring to Europe the stolen objects of gold and silver, they buried great treasures in the Coco's Island, which is situated in the Pacific Ocean between the Galapagos Islands and Costa Rica. *See Related Story 3: The Treasure of the Cocos Island.*

Because the trip from Europe to the Pacific coast of the Americas through the Strait of Magellan, at the South of Chile, was too long, the pirates wanted to conquer and control a pass along Central America. In Central America the pirates made contact with natives called the "Zambos" or "Misquitos." The pirates mixed with the Misquitos and established a community that constituted a real English Protectorate. In one opportunity a King "Misquito" was crowned in a ceremony directed by a person that represented the English Government.

The "Zambos" or "Misquitos" are the descendants of the survivors of a ship that transported African slaves and sunk close to the Atlantic coast of Nicaragua. The Africans swam to the coast and mixed with the Native American population. This coast is now known as the Mosquitia.

The English pirates saw in the Misquitos the men they needed to accomplish their plan to take an inter-oceanic passage along Central America. These people were in an area of the Atlantic coast of Nicaragua that can communicate easily with the Pacific coast of this country trough the San Juan River and the Lake of Nicaragua. The English gave those weapons, boats, and military training. With this strategy, they had the enemies of Spain inside Central America. Through the pirates, the Misquitos were in touch with the Island of Jamaica and the English.

The English were interested in this region, in the same way that many years later the American entrepreneur Cornelius Vanderbilt was, and went there and organized the Transit Company that communicated both coasts of the United States of America through Nicaragua. This company transported many people from the East Coast of the United States of America to California. Its activities finished after an inter-oceanic railroad was constructed in Panama. Cornelius Vanderbilt was the person that interested William Walker in the conquest of Central America. See *Related Story 4: William Walker.*

In 1870 the French engineer Ferdinand de Lessep directed a company that got an authorization from the Government of Colombia to initiate the construction of a canal to connect both oceans. De Lessep was not successful. Later, the Government of the United States of America under the strong leadership of its President Theodore Roosevelt, after many historical events that included the independence of Panama from Colombia, constructed the Panama Canal. See *Related Story 5: The Panama Canal.*

3   The Treasure of the Cocos Island

I heard storytellers talking about the Cocos Island and the treasures buried there by the pirates since I was a child. I always wanted to visit this island, but it is difficult to get there because there is not regular public transportation to this small tropical island.

The Cocos Island is situated about 340 miles Southwest from Costa Rica and about 400 miles northeast from the Galapagos Islands that belong to the Republic of Ecuador.

A map of this Island can fit approximately in a "rectangle" with the following coordinates: 5 degrees and 30 minutes north to 5 degrees and 34 minutes north, and 87 degrees and 1 minute west to 87 degrees and 6 minutes west.

The Cocos Island average dimensions are 4.5 miles long approximately in East West direction and 2.1 miles wide approximately in North South direction. It has an area of almost ten square miles.

The Galapagos Islands have an original, diverse and exotic flora and fauna. After visiting these islands the English scientist and writer Charles Darwin wrote its famous book "*The origin of Species.*" The Cocos Island also has a great biodiversity and exotic species. Some birds formerly found only in the Galapagos Islands have been also found in the Cocos Island.

There is not regular public transportation to Cocos Island. Some tourists go there in private boats to see its natural beauty, flora, fauna and isolated ecology. Others go there to search for the pirate's treasures that they think still could be there.

In the year 1977, when I was Vice-Minister of Natural Resources of Costa Rica, I had the opportunity to visit the Cocos Island. I needed to visit it, because we had a project to declare it a National Park and a Biological Reserve. This project, proposed to the President of Costa Rica Daniel Oduber at the end of his Administration by the Director of National Parks Engineer Alvaro Ugalde, had the strong support of the Minister of Agriculture Doctor Rodolfo Quiros.

Because it was too complicated to organize an official trip at the end of an administration in a country without navy and with only a limited Coast Guard Service, I decided to accept an invitation and joined a group of forty persons who booked in a trip organized by the Costa Rica Radio Club.

We went to the Cocos Island in a small ship which name was "El Audaz" (The Audacious.) The owner and captain of "El Audaz" was a fisherman named Lalo Mairena. He accepted to make an eight days tour to the Island. The Radio Club had to pay him the same money that he would make fishing those eight days, plus any extra costs of the trip. We thought it was a good deal.

A Friday of March at 8 pm, we departed from the port of Puntarenas and navigated in the Gulf of Nicoya in route to Cabo Blanco. That day the weather was not nice. There were heavy strong winds and a lot of rain. Traveling by ship that day was very rough because of the big waves.

Captain Mairena told us that the bad weather we had was known as "El Papagayo" and that it affected a great region of Central America. A Peruvian sailor, who was traveling with us, told us that this bad weather reminded him the one known as "Paracas" in Peru, Ecuador and other parts of the Pacific coast of South America.

This is a problem, told us Captain Mairena, now I have to take a route normal to the waves to protect the ship. I have to change the original navigation plan. Today with the help of navigation satellites, the problem that Captain Mairena mentioned would not exist. But those days we did not have this navigation technology. In the ship El Audaz we did not have radar, not radio compass equipment. The navigation equipment we had was similar to that of Christopher Columbus times.

The Captain went to the post of command and changed the ship's route. He made a lot of notes in a book, including the old route, the new route, the time of the change, the ship speed in knots, etc. I also observed that he made some lines in a map. By radio, he talked to somebody about the changes he did.

We continued traveling in bad weather for five more hours. One of the passengers, who worked in small ship construction, told me that he was afraid that this small ship of wood could not resist a longer time in that bad weather.

Suddenly the bad weather was over. The Captain went again to the command post, studied the situation, changed the route and made notes in his book and lines in his map. Now we have a route to go directly to the Cocos Island, "he told us". Some of the Radio Club members installed antennas and started communicating with their friends and radio people around the world from their radio stations that they called TIRX. They told me that these communications and the ones they will make from the island were very important, because usually there are no communications from the Cocos Island or from ships going there.

At 2 am I went to sleep. The next day, at 10 am, I made a visit to the command post and observed that the Captain was looking continuously at his book, his map, his speed meter, his clock and his compass. I noted that he reduced the speed of the ship. I asked him if something was wrong. He told me that everything was all right, but that he reduced the speed of the ship from 20 to 10 knots because he wanted to arrive to the island during the day. "It is very difficult to find this Island at night, at the new speed we will be there tomorrow morning at 7 am", said Captain Mairena.

It called my attention the great quantity of fish that jumped from the sea and flew like birds. One sailor told me that in those waters there are many schools of that fish that are called "palometas" (small doves.) I saw two dolphins escorting our ship. I wonder how they can swim at the same speed of the ship.

The sun looked like a great fireball that painted everything of yellow and golden colors, it moved slowly to the horizon, and suddenly vanished. It looked as if the sea had swallowed it.

The quiet waters allowed us to have sweet dreams. I waked up the next day at 6:30 a.m. I went to the command post and found Captain Mairena worried. "I have a concern", he told me; "we are supposed to be close to this island, but I do not see it." He gave his long distance lenses to one of the radio fans who had been in the island before. His friends call this guy "Ojo de Aguila" (Eagle Eyes) because in previous trips he has been the first person to see the island. Ojo de Aguila made a search of 360 degrees with the long distance lenses, but he did not see anything. Ojo de Aguila told me that it is very difficult to see the island from a far distance, mainly in the morning, because there are many low clouds and too much fog.

Captain Mairena reviewed all his notes and lines in his map and made a small route correction to the right. Ojo de Aguila continued looking for the island, but did not find it. One hour later, at 9 am. Ojo de Aguila, who had continued searching for the island, suddenly said with a smile, "see that shadow there, that one that looks like a dark cloud, it is the damn Island." He gave the lenses to Captain Lalo Mairena and after a watch, he said: "We made it", and he changed the ship's route directly toward the island.

Two hours later we were in the Cocos Island's Chathan Bay. The Captain told us that we were not going to disembark there, because it will be better to do that in Wafer Bay which is closer to better flat lands for camping, and where the ship will be more protected. There is also a river in that area, the Genio River, which is the longest river in the island. "We will have in this area all the water we will need," told us the Captain. After the ship El Audaz anchored in Wafer Bay, we moved to the island in small boats, with all the baggage and camping tents, radio stations and additional equipment.

In the island we found abandoned buildings and homes where the radio equipments and their antennas were installed. All the tents were installed also, and two hours later the Radio Club members were talking. They communicated with San Jose, Costa Rica, and we had the opportunity to talk with our families. We were very proud to be talking to them from the Cocos Island.

We heard the radio speakers saying TIRX, TIRX, TIRX, when the radio communications were being established with Costa Rica and the rest of Central America, North America, South America, Europe, Asia, Africa and Australia.

The cook of El Audaz, who was an African Costa Rican that was called by his crew friends "el Negro" sent us a very good supper, after which we went to bed. The next day, in the early morning, several wild pigs that were close to our tents woke us up. "Quite a big mistake was made many years ago, when these animals were brought here", said an ecologist that was in the group. They are predators of this natural paradise. We do not know when, and if these pigs were brought to this island by the pirates, or by tourists, or by the Costa Rican Government officials. It is probable that the pirates brought the pigs to the Island because they visited it frequently to get water and bury their stolen treasures, and the pigs could have been for them a source of protein to feed their crews.

A great quantity of beautiful white doves called our atten-tion. We saw also the ruins of some excavations made by people who had been there before looking for the treasures buried by the pirates many years ago.

We saw that another ship, with an American flag anchored in Wafer Bay. Twelve persons arrived to the coast, and later installed two nice big tents. They told us that they belonged to a club of entomologists from California, and that they went there to study the island insects.

The entomologists told us that in this island there are many insects not known in other parts of the world. These entomologists spent the night turning on powerful lights that attracted thousands of insects. They also told us that any entomologist that comes to this Island could identify at least one type of insect never seen before, give it his name, and include his name in the catalogs and scientific publications about entomology.

One morning, I accompanied Engineer Oton Brenes, who wanted to explore some tall rocks that were in the coast. It was not easy to get there, it was a risky tour, but we made it. Suddenly Oton Brenes fell down from a big rock mass that was about 40 feet high from the water. I was very scared for this accident; I thought that Oton could have died. Fortunately, he fell in a sea pond, and had only minor injuries. I believe it was a miracle that he survived.

It seems like another miracle, but in the group there was a doctor, and he was sailing not too far from the site where Oton fell down. He saw the accident and came to help Oton. He helped Oton to get in his boat and cured him. The doctor told us no to go to places that were too dangerous because the medical resources he had to take care of victims of accidents were very limited. I decided to return to our tents through the rocks because I did not have the stamina to make the jump that Oton did.

The next day, we went to explore the island going upstream the Genio River for the whole day. We saw excavations made by pirate treasure's hunters. We could see real nature miracles. We saw blue crabs with yellow eyes, great river shrimps, small green reptiles, iguanas, white doves, and all kinds of birds. In this trip I fell down and lost a 22-caliber gun that I had brought. We saw wild pigs running; these pigs are thin and look like dogs because they ran all the time around the island.

We did not reach it, but we could see the Iglesias Mountain, which is the tallest mountain in this island, with 2100 feet above sea level. This is a high elevation for an island with an area of about ten square miles. The Iglesias Mountain is also the tallest elevation of the Cocos plate, one of the great Earth's plates. We returned through a forest, and we found a waterfall. We found the Genio River again in a point about a mile from our tents. We saw more ruins of what looked like another excavation made by pirate treasure's hunters.

Nobody knows if the pirate treasures are still buried there. It could be that the same pirates took them out of there. It is also possible that somebody found a treasure there, but never notified the authorities, afraid, to pay taxes to his own Government, to the Government of Costa Rica, to the Government of Peru, to the Government of Spain and maybe to the United Kingdom Government. Maybe the treasure found would not be enough to pay all the taxes that those involved Governments would want.

The real treasure of the Cocos Island is its natural beauty, its biodiversity, and the abundant fisheries in its territorial waters. It is estimated that in the territorial waters of this island (126,000 square miles) the international fleet fishes more than forty thousands tons of tuna fish per year.

The next day, Captain Lalo Mairena invited us to a tour around the island. The idea was to learn more about the island and to fish if possible. One of the guys fishing, the Engineer Jimmy Vincent caught a tuna fish, when he was taking it out of the water, a shark jumped and ate almost all the tuna fish, leaving the fisherman Vincent with only the head of the tuna fish and he was very scared. Later, we saw hundreds of sharks in the water. Another fisherman caught a female shark. It was found that it had four small sharks in her womb. We also saw a great quantity of dolphins close to our ship.

We spent two more days exploring the island. One guy from Argentina killed a wild pig and cooked it for us. He was a good cook. But the pig's meat was too hard, probably because those wild pigs are running all the time. Some of the ecologists said that it would be better to kill all those pigs, and give the Island a chance to return to what it was before these pigs arrival. But other ecologists said that now it is better to leave them there because they have been there for long times, and now they are part of the ecosystem. Anyway, many things that happen in nature are by chance. And these pigs are there by chance, because some foolish people brought them.

Finally, the day to end the tour arrived. We were happy to go back home, but we were not happy for leaving the Island. During this tour we felt something special, we felt that Costa Rica was bigger, better and more beautiful because it has this Island that is a treasure lost in the Pacific Ocean. During the return trip, the weather was very good. Eight days after the departure we arrived back to the port of Puntarenas.

It is known that the President of the United States of America Franklin D. Roosevelt visited this Island frequently. He was smart going there, and for Costa Rica it was an honor when the White House asked for authorizations for these private visits of the President, which for obvious reasons were top secret. Cocos Island is a beautiful and very safe place to go.

President Roosevelt went there in 1935, in 1938 and in 1940. It seems that before World War II he liked to go there to fish, to have a summer time away from the winter and to forget for a while the complications of the management of the crisis of the Great Depression. Nobody thinks that he went there to look for the pirates buried treasures.

Maybe President Roosevelt got in that Island the stamina he later would need for his difficult mission during the following years of the II World War, when he worked long hours with the British Prime Minister Sir Winston Churchill and their military advisors looking for a strategy to defeat the Axis Powers. Probably when he got tired for the hard days of work that demanded the war against Hitler, Mussolini and Hirohito he could get some relax remembering the multicolor species of fish and the beautiful environment that he had seen in this tropical paradise.

In 1978 Cocos Island was declared, by the Costa Rican Government, a National Park, and Biological Reserve. In 1984, the marine environment within 15 kilometers from the Island was included in the National Park's protected area. In 1992, the marine area protected by the National Park was extended to 25 kilometers from the Island. Because of its educational and scientific importance and natural beauty, on December 6, 1997 the United Nations Educational, Scientific and Cultural Organization (UNESCO) declared Cocos Island a **World Heritage Site**.

4 William Walker

William Walker was born in Nashville, Tennessee in 1824. He studied in Nashville and later graduated as a medical doctor at the University of Pennsylvania. He made post graduate medical studies in Paris, France. He was also a lawyer admitted to the Louisiana Bar. There, he was also a news media man, and became editor and owner of a newspaper in New Orleans.

In 1850 William Walker went to California. In 1853, he led a group of armed men and went to Baja California where he declared himself the President of a new Republic that included the Mexican States of Sonora and Baja California. He surrendered to the Authorities of the United States of America after being accused of an illegal activity. He was judged and acquitted.

In 1855, William Walker took advantage of a difficult political situation between the Liberal and Conservative parties of Nicaragua. He accepted an invitation of the Liberal party and went to that country with a group of adventurers called filibusters. He led them and was successful capturing the City of Granada, Nicaragua.

He took the power and proclaimed himself President of Nicaragua in 1856. William Walker believed that slavery was good. He initiated a project to convert Central America in a Region that provided slaves to the United States of America. He said to the Nicaraguans that his program was the construction of an inter-oceanic canal and the development of the whole region with organized slavery. William Walker activities in Central America were supported by some people in the South of the United States of America but rejected by its government.

Costa Rica, the neighbor country at the South of Nicaragua, received with great concern the news of what was happening. The President of Costa Rica, Juan Rafael Mora, was informed that Walker's plan was to invade Costa Rica first and later to conquer Honduras, El Salvador, and Guatemala. President Mora saw that it was not convenient to wait for the arrival of Walker and his filibusters and have the battles against him in Costa Rica. He organized an army and put it under the command of generals Jose Joaquin Mora and Jose Maria Cañas.

President Mora, after many patriotic proclaims, ordered his army to depart to Nicaragua and fight in that country against the invaders William Walker and his filibusters. Among the many battles that happened, special mention deserve the battle of Santa Rosa in Costa Rica, and the battles of Rivas and San Juan del Sur in Nicaragua.

On April 11, 1856, the filibusters had made a stronghold in a place named the Meson de Guerra in the city of Rivas, Nicaragua. After heavy fire exchange, the Costa Ricans saw the necessity to take the filibusters out of the Meson de Guerra that they were occupying. The General that commanded the Costa Rican forces asked the troops: "Is there among you a volunteer who wants to go to arson the Meson de Guerra?" A soldier, with the name Juan Santamaria, gave a step forward, and said: "I will arson the Meson the Guerra, but if I get kill, you will take care of my mother, because I am her only support"

Juan Santamaria received a flamed stick and walked toward the Meson de Guerra. He reached it and was successful putting it in flames before being killed by the heavy enemy fire. The filibusters ran and abandoned their stronghold.

Many countries in the Americas have an Independence hero, like George Washington in the United States of America, Simon Bolivar in the United States of Venezuela, Jose Marti in Cuba and Jose de San Martin in Argentina. The national hero of Costa Rica is Juan Santamaria. His memory is perpetuated giving his name to the principal airport of Costa Rica.

Costa Rica does not have an Independence hero because this country never fought a war with Spain to get its independence. Costa Rica was part of the Capitania General de Guatemala. When the Capitania General de Guatemala got its Independence from Spain, on September 15, 1821, Costa Rica became part of the United Provinces of Central America; and later, for only two years, these Provinces became part of the Mexican Empire of Agustin de Iturbide; a vast empire that extended from what today is the State of Oregon in the United States of America to the border of Costa Rica with what today is the Republic of Panama. After the Iturbide Empire failed, the United Provinces of Central America became independent again. In 1848 Costa Rica declared its independence from the United Republics of Central America, a failed federation that accepted the secession of Costa Rica and the other republics without any military action.

After being defeated by the Central Americans, William Walker and the surviving filibusters went back to the United States of America where they made efforts to organize another adventure in Central America. In 1860, William

Walker arrived to Honduras with the idea of occupying this country and later Nicaragua. But an English war ship was in Honduras and ordered his crew to capture Walker, what they did. The English gave Walker and his filibusters to the Honduras Government. The Honduras Government executed them on September 12, 1860.

5   The Panama Canal

In 1513 Vasco Nuñez de Balboa discovered the "Mar del Sur" that means "Sea of the South"; he called it with this name because in Panama this Ocean, later named Pacific by Magellam, is in the South. Finally, the Spaniards had found the route Columbus was looking for to go to Japan, China and India traveling westward. This was very important.

After Balboa's discovery, the Spaniards began to think about the importance of a passage between both oceans. In those days, they transported ships in pieces from the Atlantic to the Pacific through the very primitive roads they had made. The Spaniards realized that to make a passage was just a dream given the technologies available those days for earth moving and construction.

A canal between both oceans in Panama would be about forty miles long. In Nicaragua it is possible to dig a canal of less than ten miles between the Pacific port of San Juan del Sur and the Lake of Nicaragua; and then to continue to the Atlantic through the lake and the San Juan River. It would be easier to build a canal in Nicaragua for small ships than in Panama, but not one that would allow the passage of big ships.

The Nicaraguan Canal would have the limitations that the San Juan River has for navigation, mainly when it reaches the Pacific Ocean, close to Costa Rica's Barra del Colorado. It could be more difficult and expensive to correct the navigation characteristics of the San Juan River to allow the passage of big ships than to build the Canal in Panama.

In the seventeenth and eighteenth centuries, the Kings of Spain order studies about possible passages. But it was only in the nineteen century, after heavy equipment for earth moving and construction were available, that engineers thought of an inter-oceanic passage as a real possibility.

In 1882, the French engineer Ferdinand de Lessep, who had participated in the construction of the Suez Canal in Egypt, signed an agreement with the Government of Colombia and initiated the construction of the Panama Canal. He had many problems there. The labor force became sick with malaria, yellow fever, dengue, acute diarrheas and other tropical diseases. The Ferdinand de Lessep Company finished in bankruptcy.

In 1902, the United States of America wanted to build the Panama Canal. President Theodore Roosevelt, a man of great resolution, got an agreement with the Government of Colombia that was later rejected by the Colombian Senate; but President Roosevelt wanted to build the canal.

A French engineer, Philippe Bunau-Varilla, who had worked for Ferdinand de Lessep, joined a group of Panamanians who were talking about independence from Colombia. They asked for help to President Theodore Roosevelt. In November 3, 1903, Panama declared its independence from Colombia. The Government of the United States of America recognized the new country immediately; and the American Navy was there with several ships and ready to protect the new Nation.

The Panama Government, still under formation, sent Mr. Philippe Bunau-Varilla to discuss an agreement for the construction of the Panama Canal. An agreement was reached, and the Panama Canal Company initiated its activities. However, it was a serious legal problem: when Mr. Bunau-Varilla signed this agreement, no Panamanian was present. Mr. Bunau-Varilla had been sent by the Panamanian Government to discuss a possible contract, not to negotiate it or to sign it. This is the original sin of the Panama Canal, and probably the reason that moved the Government of the United States of America to sign a new agreement and to transfer the Canal Zone and the Canal to the Republic of Panama in the year 2000, when the "Manifest Destiny," the "Big Stick" and the "Dollar Diplomacy" policies were supposed to be over.

President Jimmy Carter, who signed with Panamanian President Omar Torrijos the agreements to give this Canal to Panama, understood that giving it to Panama would eliminate a source of friction between the United States of America and the countries of Latin America, and the anger that the new generation of Panamanians had about the way in which the Canal Treaty was signed.

Despite the political and legal problems discussed before, the Panama Canal was a great achievement. The United States of America must be proud of the engineers that designed, constructed and operated this world marvel. It was not an easy task. Two Chief Engineers who made great contributions to the project, including important modifications to the original design and construction plan, resigned during the construction of the Canal. President Roosevelt became furious for the resignations and nominated a military Chief Engineer who would be subject to military rules and discipline. He finished the Canal.

Because building a sea level canal would require a tremendous earth moving, the American Engineers designed an artificial lake (Gatun Lake) and locks to put the ships up in this Lake, and locks to put the ships down in the other ocean. An important part of the earth moved to make the canal was used to construct the dam used to create the Gatun Lake.

Knowing the problems that the French have had previously, the Americans sent medical doctors, epidemiologists, entomologists and sanitary engineers to improve the sanitary conditions before the heavy construction was initiated. During the occupation of Cuba in the war with Spain, the Americans had learned that malaria, dengue and yellow fever are diseases transmitted by mosquitoes and how to control them. They also knew the importance of safe water supply and adequate wastewater disposal. Admiral William Gorgas, an army medical officer, was sent to Panama to direct the sanitary, environmental and health conditions improvement. The United States of America initiated the heavy construction stage of the Panama Canal Project only after the environmental, sanitary and health conditions were improved.

However, despite the improvements in sanitation and diseases control, many people died during the construction of the Panama Canal, most of them in accidents during the construction, but some of them from tropical diseases that at the beginning had not been successfully eradicated.

On August 15, 1914, the first ship traveled across the Panama Canal, but because of the complications of the First World War, and some landslides and operational difficulties, the normal operation of the canal was not initiated immediately. The Panama Canal was open officially in 1920. The citizens of the United States of America were very proud, because they made it. The dream of Christopher Columbus was finally a reality. Now it is possible to go from Europe to Japan, China and India navigating westward. No longer is necessary to go South trough the Magellan Strait.

The Panama Canal was since the beginning open for the navigation of all the countries of the world. It had helped a lot to the economic development of many countries, including Colombia, the country that lost Panama. We can say that to give this great service to the whole World Navigation, one Country, Colombia, lost her daughter Panama, and this daughter country, Panama, accepted to divide its territory in two parts. Many people gave their lives in the construction of this World Marvel.

President Theodore Roosevelt visited Panama during the construction of the canal. The people of Latin America did not like him for the intervention of the United States of America in the Independence of Panama, and for the illegal agreement he made to build the Canal. But Latin American people admired him for his strong support to this mission of progress almost impossible; and because he knew that the United States of America was the only country with the capacity to construct it.

People around the Americas and the world were happy with the Canal, because it was going to be very useful for all mankind. President Theodore Roosevelt made mistakes, but he made the canal; maybe in the only way it could be done.

The Panamanian struggle to recover the territory of the Canal Zone started in the 1950s, with fights between Panamanian students and "Zonians" as they called the American students that were the children of the American personnel of the Canal

Zone. The Zonians put American flags in the Canal Zone, but during the night Panamanian students changed them for Panamanian flags. One day some of the Panamanian students were killed, and the Panama Canal crisis began.

In 1969, when Omar Torrijos arrived to power in Panama it was not important news. Another General became the ruler and dictator of another Central American Republic, something that in the turbulent Central America of those days was not news.

However, President Omar Torrijos won rapid the respect and the admiration of the people of Panama. With his talent and leadership Omar Torrijos substituted his lack of political experience; he also demonstrated to his people that he was a patriot. He did not look for advice from the dictators of his time like Nicaragua's Anastasio Somoza or Chile's Augusto Pinochet. He became a good friend of democratic leaders, like Costa Rica's Daniel Oduber, Colombia's Alfonso Lopez, Venezuela's Carlos Andres Perez and Spain's Adolfo Suarez.

Omar Torrijos experienced through time a metamorphosis toward democracy that made him unhappy for the undemocratic origin of his regimen. "I am a convict, converse and confess dictator," he said in one opportunity.

President Omar Torrijos united the Panamanian people, who supported his nationalist thesis to recover the Panama's sovereignty over his country's whole territory. In his speeches struggling for the recovery of the Panama Canal Zone he said "de pie o muertos, nunca de rodillas" ("standing or dead, never kneeling down".)

Some Omar Torrijos enemies said that he was a leftist and a communist; others said that he was just one more rightist Latin American dictator. His answer was "ni con la derecha, ni con la izquierda, con las dos manos por Panama" ("neither with the left nor with the right, with both hands for Panama".)

What most favor President Omar Torrijos image was his role as negotiator. Through persuasion and with his ability to get support for the Panamanian cause inside and outside of the Americas, President Torrijos convinced the Government of the United States of America that it was necessary to initiate a process to give back the Panama Canal Zone to Panama.

President Omar Torrijos achievement was too big. He got the recovery of the most strategic territory in the Americas, by a small Country, trough negotiation and dialogue with the most powerful country of the world. If we evaluate leaders for the results they get, we have to arrive to the conclusion that President Omar Torrijos was a great leader.

When President Jimmy Carter signed the agreement to give the Panama Canal Zone and the Panama Canal back to Panama, he did what was just and necessary. The territory where the canal was constructed always belonged to Panama. The United States of America could not get this territory through an agreement signed by a no authorized French citizen.

To facilitate the transfer of the Canal from the United States of America to Panama, the Panama Canal Commission was created in 1979. This Commission had nine members and was integrated by five Americans and four Panamanians. It existed for a transition period of twenty years in which

American personnel of the Canal was substituted gradually by Panamanian personnel.

In the year 2000 the Panamanians assumed the full operation of the Canal. It has continued working fine. The Americans made a fine job training the Panamanians.

Some Americans, the defenders of "Manifest Destiny", were disappointed when the agreement to transfer the Panama Canal to Panama was signed. They said that the big investment made there by the United States of America could not be lost that way; that the Panamanians had no capacity to operate the Canal. They considered that it does not matters that the Latin American people said that the United States of America is a Country with not respect for international law, and that it is better to handle those countries with a "Big Stick". The American people that think that way are responsible for the anti-American movements in Latin America. It is for them, for some oil companies and some rough developers that in Latin America are winning elections leaders like Venezuela's Hugo Chaves, Nicaragua's Daniel Ortega, Bolivia's Evo Morales and others.

The Panamanians believe that the United States of America recovered the investment made in the Panama Canal, with a very good rate of return, during the years the Americans operated it. They also say that the most important natural resource that Panama has is its geographical location and that they contributed with it during eighty years. They believe that they paid for the Canal.

For the Latin American People, President Jimmy Carter is considered the best President that the United States of America has ever had. He is a good man. He is a decent man. He is a gentleman. He has respect for international law. He transformed the intervention of the Panama Canal into the joint venture of the Panama Canal.

We admire President Theodore Roosevelt for his achievement in a mission almost impossible and for the construction of a World Marvel, and we respect President Jimmy Carter because he corrected President Theodore Roosevelt mistakes.

Since there are now many ships bigger than those of 1905 when the canal designs were made, the government of Panama, together with the government of the United States of America have an agreement to increase the capacity of the canal for today's great ships. Because of the great investments involved in this new project, the People of Panama were consulted, in an election, before the agreement could be signed. There is a big difference when we compare this new agreement with the first one in which no Panamanian participated.

In September 2007, the construction to increase the capacity of the Panama Canal was initiated. The Panamanian President Martin Torrijos, the son of former Panamanian President Omar Torrijos, invited President Jimmy Carter to the inauguration of the works. He also invited the Presidents of Colombia and the Central American countries to this inauguration.

6   The Commonwealth of Puerto Rico

Puerto Rico is a beautiful island in the Caribbean that was called Borinquen by the Native Americans. It was discovered by Christopher Columbus in his second voyage to the Americas in 1493, and he claimed it for the kingdom of Spain.

Juan Ponce de Leon, a Spanish explorer that had accompanied Christopher Columbus in his second voyage, was sent as Governor of this island from 1510 to 1512. Being Governor of Puerto Rico, Juan Ponce de Leon heard stories from the island Native Americans who told him that North from the island of Cuba *a big and rich country existed.* The Native Americans also told Ponce de Leon that in that country there was a fountain of the eternal youth and that people who take baths in that fountain become forever young.

Ponce de Leon got authorization from the King of Spain to explore the region north from Cuba and discovered the peninsula of Florida in March 27, 1512. On April 27, 1513 he landed close to what today is the Fort of San Agustin. That day was an Easter Sunday that in Spanish is "Pascua Florida" and he gave the name of Florida to that land that he thought was an island. He navigated in Southward direction and discovered what today are known as the Florida Keys. Then he traveled back to Puerto Rico. Consequently, we can say that Juan Ponce de Leon discovered the territory of the United States of America.

It would be nice to say that in 1493 Christopher Columbus discovered part of what it is today the territory of the United States of America. Taking into consideration that the free associated Commonwealth of Puerto Rico belongs to the

United States of America, we could say that; but the problem is that Puerto Rico is not an American State. We can say only that, in 1493, Christopher Columbus discovered Puerto Rico that is today a free associated Commonwealth of the United States of America.

Juan Ponce de Leon traveled again to Florida to conquer and colonize it in 1521. He landed in West Florida with 200 men, but found unfriendly Native Americans that attacked them. Ponce de Leon was seriously injured in this fight and the Spaniards decided to go back to their ships. The expedition traveled to Cuba, where Juan Ponce de Leon died a short time later.

Probably the Florida Native Americans did not know that the Spaniards had killed Montezuma in Mexico; and they did not know that the Spaniards will kill Atahualpa in Peru. However; we have to recognize that they were not so wrong fighting the Spaniards.

Puerto Rico became a territory of the United States of America after its war with Spain in 1898, almost four hundred years after it was conquered by Spain.

After more than a century of being a territory of the United States of America, Puerto Rico still continues under the United States of America sovereignty without Statehood and without independence.

In 1946, the Government of the United States of America nominated Jesus Piñero as the first Puerto Rican Governor of the island. In 1949 Luis Muñoz Marin became the first governor elected by the people of Puerto Rico under the status of free associated Commonwealth.

There have been several voting processes in Puerto Rico to decide its future status, and the people of Puerto Rico have voted to continue with its actual free associated Commonwealth status. There are many reasons for this preference, including that Puerto Rico has the markets of the United States of America open to its products; Puerto Ricans do no need to get a visa to go to the United States of America, and they can go to live in any State because they are American citizens; the per capita income of Puerto Rico is higher than the ones of the other Latin American countries; and Puerto Ricans do not pay some of the Federal taxes that the Americans have to pay.

The status of Puerto Rico is not good for the Image of the United States of America in the world and in Latin America. A country that initiated its independent life with a revolution against an empire should not have a territory that could be called a colony.

If we believe like President John F. Kennedy that the true power of the United States of America comes from democratic ideas, and not from military might, we should be putting more attention to the status of Puerto Rico or to the status of Washington D.C., where they have taxation without representation.

The Puerto Ricans, who live in Puerto Rico, cannot vote in the elections for the President of the United States of America, a President that makes decisions that affect them. Democratic leaders are supposed to rule only over peoples that have participated in their election. The Congress of the United States of America passes laws that affect Puerto Ricans, but Puerto Ricans do not have representatives that can vote when these laws are passed. Democratic legislators are supposed to pass laws that rule only over people that have participated in their elections.

After becoming a territory of the United States of America, Puerto Rico has had soldiers and military personnel cooperating with all the military efforts of America. Many Puerto Ricans had made the ultimate sacrifice for America. They have died fighting in wars decided by American Presidents or Congresses that were elected without the votes of the people of Puerto Rico.

The status of Puerto Rico represents more a problem to the United States of America than for the Puerto Ricans. The people from Puerto Rico look happy. They are very good people and they are not looking for trouble, however there is not consensus among all the Puerto Ricans about what status is the best for their country.

To declare the independence of Puerto Rico probably would be simple. It is possible that the Congress of the United States of America would accept it easily, but for many years the economy of Puerto Rico has been adjusted to an open market with the United States of America, and to receive big investments from American companies. When Puerto Ricans compare their economic situation with that of their neighbors in the Caribbean, they do not fill that independence would be good for them.

On the other hand, to become another State of the United States of America could be a better possibility for Puerto Rico. But it would be a serious problem if the Puerto Ricans vote to be another State of the Union and the Congress of the United States of America do not accept that decision.

The only way to get the statehood for Puerto Rico is that the government of the United States of America take a resolution establishing that Puerto Rico can continue as a free associated Commonwealth, but that if the people of Puerto Rico decide in a free voting process that they want to be an State of the United States of America, they are welcome. Without a previous and clear pronunciation like this, it would be unwise for the Puerto Ricans to vote to become one State of the Union, because the decision does not belong only to them.

To get the Statehood for Puerto Rico is not a problem easy to solve because it would be the only Spanish speaking State in the United States of America. Some people in the United States of America are afraid of that because they do not want to have a bilingual country. They are the same people that are afraid of the waves of immigrants from Mexico and the rest of Latin America. They say that in a country with the diversity of the United States of America the English language is the glue that keeps the pieces united. But the reality is that the United States of America has been a bilingual country for many years.

Many people speak Spanish and English in Puerto Rico. Almost all the professionals read and study in English books. Puerto Rico has now a delegate, with voice but no vote in the House of Representatives of the Congress of the United States of America. He speaks and understands English. If Puerto Rico would some day have two Senators and more Representatives they would have to be fluent in English, because it would not be practical to have a bilingual Congress just for one State that speaks Spanish, if the other fifty speak English.

However, interpreters could be used if necessary.

There are bilingual countries like Canada and Belgium that work fine. Switzerland is a country with four languages that works very well. In Spain not everybody speak Spanish. In the United Kingdom not everybody speak English. India is a country with many languages.

The Americans that are worry because there are people speaking Spanish in the United States of America should know all these facts.

7 The Cold War in Central America

The Cold War affected the Central American countries in a way that was not so cold. Many Nicaraguans, Salvadorians and other Central Americans are in the United States of America today because the United States of America and the Soviet Union went there to fight the Cold War in their territory.

More than 250,000 Central Americans were killed and more were wounded in the Central American cold war, many of them civilians, women and children. Costa Rica received many refugees, Honduras had the Contras, Guatemala had many combats of government forces against rebel groups in rural areas and against communist guerrillas, but the most affected countries were Nicaragua and El Salvador.

Nicaragua

Nicaragua is a strategic country because it has an inter-oceanic canal possibility. In 1912, there was political violence in Nicaragua. The United States of America Government sent the Marines to Nicaragua and occupied the country. The idea was to stabilize Nicaragua, a country with one of the alternatives for the inter-oceanic canal that the Government of the United States of America wanted to build. The American troops stayed in Nicaragua until 1925, but after they left the political violence started again.

We have to understand that the inter-oceanic canal is very important even today, but it was more important when aviation, railroads and highways had not been developed to the levels they later reached in the United States of America.

In 1926, the marines arrived again to Nicaragua and stayed there until 1933. In this second intervention the Americans had to fight a group of rebels organized under the leadership of Cesar Augusto Sandino.

When the Americans left Nicaragua they had organized the Nicaragua National Guard under the command of General Anastasio Somoza. In 1936, Somoza took the power and initiated the Somoza dynasty. He named the more important street of the Capital City, Managua, with the name of Franklin D. Roosevelt. The Somoza dynasty with Anastasio Somoza "The First" and his sons Luis and General Anastasio Somoza "The second" ruled Nicaragua during 43 years. During their dynasty, they made a few elections and gave the power to puppet leaders for short periods to simulate that Nicaragua had a democracy.

The Somozas liked to have interventions in other countries. In 1948, they sent 2000 troops to Costa Rica, and in 1961 Somoza collaborated with the United States Central Intelligence Agency in the training of the Cubans that participated in the Bahia de Cochinos attack against the Cuban Regimen of Fidel Castro.

The Somozas were brutal dictators. President Franklin D. Roosevelt, talking about General Anastasio Somoza "The First", said in one opportunity "Somoza is a son of a bitch, but he is our son of a bitch." The problem with this type of policy is that when the United States of America said that they support democracy and freedom in the world, the

Nicaraguans do not believe that. This is the reason why the Nicaraguans have supported the Sandinistas.

The Soviet Union took advantage of this situation, and helped the Nicaraguans who organized the "Frente Sandinista de Liberacion Nacional" (FSLN) (or Sandinista Front for National Liberation) to fight against the Somoza regimen in the 1960s. The majority of the Nicaraguan people were not communist, but they supported that somebody put an end to the Somoza family dictatorship that was installed there by the intervention of the United States of America.

The reaction of the Somoza regimen against the Sandinista war was brutal, to the point that the government killed and injured many civil people, including television, newspaper and other media workers. American reporters were there and informed about the situation. Some American reporters were victims of this situation. Somoza regimen lost the support of the United States of America government after President Jimmy Carter established policies to protect human rights worldwide. General Somoza "The Second" did not understand how this could happen. He had been always loyal to the United States of America and he was a West Point graduate.

The President Jimmy Carter administration understood that the interventions in Central America of the two Presidents Roosevelt, Theodore and Franklin D. during inter-oceanic canal days were wrong. The acquisition of the Panama Canal Zone by President Theodore Roosevelt was done in a wrong way, and the installation of the Somoza dictatorship by President Franklin D. Roosevelt was another big mistake. It seems that during the inter-oceanic canal days fever the American government forgot for a while the principles of international law and the ideals of the American Founding Fathers. Those were the days of the "Manifest Destiny", the "Dollar Diplomacy" and of the "Big Stick" policies.

The Somoza Regimen became weak after the sandinistas war started, after several natural disasters occurred including earthquakes, floods and hurricanes, and after General Anastasio Somoza "The Second" suffered a heart attack.

In 1978, a Sandinista command directed by Eden Pastora known as "Comandante Cero" (Zero Commandant) took hostage the Nicaraguan Congress. The regimen looked very weak after this attack and its negotiations with the Sandinistas. In July 1979 the Sandinistas took power in Nicaragua and the country moved from a rightist dictatorship to a leftist dictatorship.

After Ronald Reagan became President of the United States of America in 1981, the relations of this country with the Sandinistas deteriorated rapidly. The support of the Soviet Union to the Sandinistas was evident, and the Sandinistas support to leftist revolutionaries in other Central American Countries was obvious.

In 1984, the Sandinistas made an election in which the traditional political parties of Nicaragua did not participate. The Sandinista leader Daniel Ortega was elected President of Nicaragua and his party won the majority in Congress. He received a great support from Cuba and the Soviet Union.

A group of Nicaraguans, some of them former followers of the Somozas went to Honduras and initiated a contra-revolution against the Sandinistas. They were called "the Contras." President Reagan called them "Freedom Fighters" and helped them. But the money to help the Contras came from illegal transactions with Iran. Because the help to the Contras was illegal, these activities gave origin to the Iran-Contra Scandal that caused many headaches to President Reagan.

The leaders of Latin America had a great concern for the situation in Nicaragua, where the Soviet Union and the United States of America were contributing with the weapons and the munitions, and the Nicaraguans were contributing with the casualties.

In 1990, after a peace effort promoted by the Central American Presidents, known as the Arias Plan, there were free elections in Nicaragua. Daniel Ortega, the Sandinista leader lost the elections. Doña Violeta Barrios de Chamorro, the widow of the owner of a newspaper in Nicaragua who was assassinated by the Somoza regimen, won the elections.

Finally Nicaragua had an elected democratic Government. Doña Violeta governed Nicaragua like a grandmother. She saw all the Nicaraguans, rich or poor, leftists or rightists as her children and grandchildren. Finally Nicaragua had peace for a while.

Nicaragua Intervention in Costa Rica

In 1948, Somoza sent two thousand Nicaraguan National Guards to Costa Rica under the command of Colonel Tijerino to support the government of Costa Rican President, his friend Teodoro Picado, who did not recognize that his political party had lost the Costa Rica's presidential elections.

The Costa Rican communist leader, Manuel Mora, a man with great influence in the Costa Rican Government, convinced Teodoro Picado that if he gives the power to the Chief of the "right wing" party that won the elections, Otilio Ulate, all the social advances of Costa Rica would be lost. On the other hand, Somoza wanted another dictatorship in Costa Rica because Costa Rica democratic tradition was a problem for him.

A Costa Rican leader, Jose Figueres organized a revolution against the Teodoro Picado regimen, defeated his army and group of communists that supported him. Figueres defeated also Somoza's two thousand National Guards. The Nicaragua's leader of the troops sent to Costa Rica by Somoza, Colonel Tijerino, died in this fight.

It looks like a contradiction, but Figueres had to fight against a rightist Somoza's National Guard army and a communist leftist army. Those were the forces that supported Teodoro Picado regimen. It is difficult to understand, but in politics sometimes the "heat" and the "cold" join forces to work together.

After the 1948 revolution was won, Jose Figueres called to elections for an Assembly that wrote a new Constitution. He also called for a new election of Congress because the communists had burned all the electoral material of the previous Congress election. After eighteen months of Figueres transition rule, the elected President Otilio Ulate was installed. The social advances of Costa Rica were held and improved. Costa Rica's democracy continued strong and without interruptions after this incident.

El Salvador

At the beginning of the Twentieth Century the economy of El Salvador improved with the production and exportation of great quantities of coffee. However, the distribution of the income did not reach the popular classes because land tenure was inadequate.

The wealth of the country was in the hands of a few families. This was a cause of political unrest. On the other hand, El Salvador had a concentration of capital in a group of persons that were very good entrepreneurs and industrialized the country rapidly. The social situation improved with the better salaries of the industrial workers. But the concentration of the capital in a few hands in a country with limited territory was a source of problems.

In 1930, a Labor Party was organized in El Salvador to protect the interest of the working class and the poor people. Alberto Masferrer was the leader of this political movement. He was a moderate leader who made demands to the oligarchy and wanted to educate them about the social responsibility of the capital. He fought for the right of workers to establish labor unions and organize strikes. This year the Labor Party organized by Masferrer won the elections, and Arturo Araujo became President of El Salvador. Araujo was a member of the coffee grower's families, but he had a great social sensibility and wanted to help the people in need and the poor.

The economic situation was difficult; it was the time of the great world depression. Farabundo Marti, the leader of the communist party offered a revolution to take the land from the rich and to give it to the peasants and poor.

The rich looked for the support of the military. In December 1931, General Maximiliano Hernandez Martinez took the power and put the elected President Arturo Araujo out of office. Since the beginning of the dictatorship of Hernandez Martinez, the leftist leader Farabundo Marti organized the workers and the peasants against the Government. The country was in a revolution where thousands of peasants were killed by the military forces of Hernandez Martinez who continued in power until 1944, when other militaries took the power.

The government continued ruled by more moderate militaries that authorized political parties and labor unions. Because of the difficult economic situation, many Salvadorians began to emigrate to neighbor Honduras and other countries, including the United States of America.

More than 300,000 Salvadorians were in Honduras in 1969 and started having many problems with the People of Honduras. The government of this country wanted to take the Salvadorians out of Honduras.

A war between El Salvador and Honduras started after an incident happened in a stadium during a soccer match between Honduras and El Salvador. It was called the Soccer War.

After the Soccer War many Salvadorians that lived in Honduras had to go back to El Salvador, a country that was in a social crisis and where the fight of the communists for the power became more violent.

In 1979, when the Sandinistas ended the Somoza's dictatorship, the Salvadorian military became nervous because military help for the Salvadorian communists, sent by the Soviet Union, started arriving from Nicaragua. The communist organized a guerrilla against the government with the name Frente Farabundo Marti de Liberacion Nacional (FMLN) (Farabundo Marti National Liberation Front.)

In 1980, the Christian Democratic party agreed to cooperate with the military Junta ruling the Country, and Jose Napoleon Duarte became the leader in that Junta. Despite the presence of the civil leader Duarte, he could not control the military and many crimes and violence continued in the country, including the assassination of Bishop Arturo Romero.

President Reagan decided to bring support to El Salvador government in a Policy that he called "Symmetry." He said that if the Soviet Union is supporting Salvadorian communists in their war against the Salvadorian government, the United States of America has to help the Salvadorian government.

In 1984, Duarte became President of El Salvador. After many years of military rulers, finally El Salvador had a Government with a Civil President. The support of the United States helped the Duarte Government. But the civil war continued. The FMLN, with better weapons and more munitions and resources, sent by the Sandinistas were fighting hard. The situation became more complicated when a strong earthquake destroyed many cities in El Salvador and President Duarte got sick with cancer.

In 1987, the President of Costa Rica Oscar Arias, with great concern for the war in Nicaragua and El Salvador, proposed a Central America Peace Plan. This Plan was accepted and signed by Jose Napoleon Duarte, the Sandinistas and other Peace Plan participants. Oscar Arias got later the Pease Novel Price for his contribution to the efforts to pacify Central America.

After the war, the economic and social situation in El Salvador and Nicaragua became too deteriorated. Many people from these countries migrated to the United States of America, Costa Rica, Spain, Mexico and other countries.

FOURTH PART: POETRY

I CAN FEEL GOD'S PRESENCE

God:
Infinite mass of Spirit
with no origin or end.
No human mind can know where
is Your space or Your limit.

I cannot see God.
I cannot touch Him.
But I know He exists,
which gives me great hope.

I can feel God's presence,
my spirit is part of Him.
In any human being
He stays always present.

We cannot hear Him;
but we feel His infinity
which no human have seen.

We cannot smell Him,
but His perpetual mercy
we can always feel.

I GAVE YOU ALL MY HEART

(To my wife Agnes Giovanna Bartorelli)

Despite I gave you all my heart,
I was too short expressing it.
My love for you was like a heat
that took my life really apart.

Now I realize. I was too hard.
Lost in the drug of my profession,
I worked hard for the perfection.
I didn't listen to your heart.

Because my love is like pure gold;
I will forever have the hope
of a celestial mercy and love
coming from you and from the Lord.

THE VISIT OF ELIAN GONZALES [1]

Like Juan Ponce de Leon
to Florida he came
to continue the game
of visiting this region.

His mother her life gave
to give him freedom here,
and she has to stay there
with the sea as a grave.

His parent's presence feels.
That explains his smile.
This is not a surprise,
because his great skills.

Wiser than relatives,
lawyers and politicians;
like a master of magicians
ignores them and forgives.

Then he went back home
to his nice Island Country.
Out of that Dade County
he continues with hope.

[1]   Elian Gonzalez was rescued from a shipwreck close to Florida in the year 2000 when
    he was five years old. Unfortunately his mother perished in the trip. Members of
    the Miami Cuban community took care of him. Elian's father, who was in Cuba,
    wanted his child back and the Cuban government supported him in this effort.
    The American Judiciary and the American Justice Department decided to send
    Elian back to Cuba. The Miami Cubans who took care of him said that they
    would not give the child to the American Authorities, because his mother gave her
    life to bring him to freedom. The President William J. Clinton Administration
    sent law enforcement officials to take the child and gave him to his father who had
    traveled from Cuba to bring him back home. Many Americans did not like to see
    people doing politics with this tragedy and this little boy fate.

THE COCOS ISLAND

In the top of a plate[2]
and lost in the Pacific,
this island is terrific
and a wonderful gate.

I saw a beautiful dove
and some full color fishes,
as a professor teaches,
this is good land for love.

I have learned it now:
the sharks eat tuna fish;
to catch them is my wish
but I do not know how.

Please don't tell me when
that bad mosquitoes came
to play their dirty game
in this so nice Eden.

Its nice coral formation
and its beautiful beaches
satisfy all my wishes
for a happy vacation.

I will look for a treasure
buried by a pirate;
even if I do it late
to find it is a pleasure.

[2] The little Cocos Island is the only land above sea level in the Cocos Plate, which is a geological plate that gives origin to many Central America Pacific coast tectonic earthquakes when it interacts with the Caribbean plate.

INTERFAITH PRAYER

God:
Infinite mass of spirit
without origin or end
no human mind can knows where
is your space or your limit.

We pray for the world and all mankind.
You are only one. All want You.
All love You.
All fear You.

God, Dios, Allah, Yave, Almighty
You are the only God,
the God of all believers.
Help us to fight hate.
Have pity of us and give us peace.

Who looks for You is always blessed,
even if he calls You with other name,
even if he has another faith.

We pray and ask your mercy
for those who don't know You,
or in You do not believe.

THE IMMIGRANTS

Why they left land and love
and came to be heart broken?
Maybe they were forgotten,
but never lost their hope
in the land where they did move.

They work hard under the sun
as good rangers with a gun;
as drivers from somewhere
or bringing goods anywhere,
where people may have fun.

One day a tall construction
other day in a long bridge;
take great risks at a tall ridge
or help in the destruction
of a bad sewer obstruction.

Some folks don't like them,
I these people undocumented.!
They want all them deported,
despite they don't know when,
despite they don't know where.

FINAL COMMENTS

I was born in Costa Rica in 1934 and I spent my childhood and youth there. I remember very well that in the early 1940s everybody was afraid of the menace that the axis powers led by Hitler, Mussolini and Hirohito represented to the world. I remember Nazi Germany and what it called its "preemptive wars to protect the fatherland" and the occupation of many European countries by the Nazi regimen. I also remember the occupation of many Asian countries by the Japanese Empire, and the occupation of some African countries by Fascist Italy.

I remember Prime Minister Winston Churchill radio speeches making the world aware of the Axis Powers project to conquer the whole world. Under these circumstances the President of the United States of America Franklin Delano Roosevelt arrived to the conclusion that only the United States of America could save the world from the Axis powers domination project.

I remember President Roosevelt radio speeches promoting a Great Alliance to fight the Axis Powers and how the Latin American countries participated in that effort with their natural resources and logistic support capacities. The United States of America became the country that saved the whole world from the global totalitarian project of the Axis Powers. Everybody was happy in Latin America, and we learned to see the United States of America as our big brother and as a good neighbor.

After the defeat of the Axis Powers by America and the allied countries, the Soviet Union initiated the conquest of countries as part of a global communist totalitarian project. The United States of America again took the leadership against this global domination project and stopped the Soviet Union after a long cold war.

During the cold war some Latin American countries like Cuba, Chile, Guatemala and Nicaragua became allied of the Soviet Union, at least for a while, and almost in all the Latin American countries were communist parties that supported the Soviet Union plans for a worldwide communist domination. But a great majority of the people of Latin America supported the American efforts to stop the Soviet Union because they did not want a totalitarian regimen in their countries.

After the collapse of the Soviet Union the relations between the United States of America and the Latin American countries are mainly commercial. At the beginning of the third millennium there is not longer the friendship and common ideals that existed during the Franklin D. Roosevelt and John F. Kennedy days. There are troubling situations like the communist movement led by Venezuelan President Hugo Chaves, which is an anachronism.

When I was a Latin American teenager I saw The United States of America as the country that saved the world. Today Latin America teenagers see the United States of America in a different way. They see America as a superpower that originated a world economic crisis attacking Iraq in an unnecessary preemptive war.

The United States of America is building a wall in its border with Mexico. Many people in Latin America see this wall as an unfriendly attitude of the United States of America toward them.

Something has to be done to improve the relations between the countries of the Americas because they have the same values, the same heritage and a common destine. I hope that this book can help to have a better understanding between the North and the South of the Americas.

Sources of Information

Several sources of information have been used in the preparation of this book. The most important are:
La Nacion (Costa Rica)
The Washington Post
Time Magazine
US News and World Report Magazine
Encyclopedia Americana
Encyclopedia Britannica
Encyclopedia Encarta
Pirenne, Jacques. Historia Universal: las grandes corrientes de la historia. Editorial Éxito, S.A. Barcelona, 1973.
TELEVISION: CNN, FOX TV, MSNBC, PBS.
WIKIPEDIA, WEBOPEDIA

Books Consulted

Garrison, Ginger. ISLA DEL COCO FISHES. 2000. Editorial INBio. Apdo. Postal 22-3100, Santo Domingo, Heredia, Costas Rica.
Loewenhein, Francis L.; Langley, Harold D; Jonas, Manfred. ROOSEVELT AND CHURCHILL. Their Secret Wartime Correspondence. 1975. Saturday Review Press/ E.P. Dutton & Co Inc.. New York.
Saenz, Rodolfo F. CARIARI. 1982, Editorial Texto. San Jose, Costa Rica.
Seward, Desmond. NAPOLEON AND HITLER. A Comparative Biography. 1988. The Penguin Group. Viking Penguin Inc. ,40 west 23rd Street New York, New York 10010.
Veregin, Howard. GOODE'S WORLD ATLAS, 21st

Edition. Rand Mc.Nally

Wilson, Vincent Jr. THE BOOK OF GREAT AMERICAN DOCUMENTS. 1998, American History Research Associates, Box 140, Brookeville, Maryland.

About the Author of this Book

Rodolfo F. Saenz

Rodolfo F. Saenz was born in San Jose, Costa Rica, in September 23, 1934. He studied civil engineering at the University of Costa Rica, Ground Water Development at the University of Minnesota, and completed a Post Graduate Program in Sanitary Engineering at the IHE-Delft, The Netherlands. He is a Member of the American Society of Civil Engineers (ASCE). He is fluent in English and Spanish and became a U.S. Citizen in February 2003.

He worked during sixteen years for the Pan American Health Organization, the Regional Office for the Americas of the World Health Organization, a Specialized Agency of the United Nations, in Ecuador, Peru and the United States of America. He worked fourteen years in various agencies of the Government of Costa Rica, including two years as advisor to the President of Costa Rica, and two years as Vice-Minister of Natural Resources of Costa Rica.

He was professor of Sanitary Engineering and of Hydraulic Works, for ten years at the School of Civil Engineering of the University of Costa Rica. He was lecturer and consultant at the Pan American Center of Sanitary Engineering and

Environmental Sciences in Lima, Peru, during eight years. He wrote a book in Spanish with the title "Cariari." 1 He has also produced many technical books and publications in the field of sanitary and environmental engineering, most of which can be seen in: Saenz Forero Rodolfo in:

http://www.cepis.ops-oms.org.

Since 1988, Rodolfo F. Saenz lives in Rockville, Maryland with his wife Agnes Giovanna Bartorelli and their daughter Marianella. Their daughters Carmen Isabel and Agnes Giovanna Saenz also live in Rockville, Maryland. Their son Gaston Saenz lives in San Jose, Costa Rica, with his wife Rosa and their children Mario, Gaston and Aranzazu.